The New Reef Aquarium:

Setup, Care and Compatibility

Guidance from an Aquarium Authority
By Laurren Schmoyer

Copyright © 2014 by Aquatic Experts
Published 2014 by Aquatic Experts
All rights reserved.

No part of this publication may be reproduced or transmitted in any form or by any means, mechanical or electronic, including photocopying and recording, or by any information storage and retrieval system, without permission in writing from the publisher.

http://www.aquaticexperts.com
If you have any questions email us at
customerservice@aquaticexperts.com

About the Author

Laurren Schmoyer owned and operated an aquarium store for over 25 years; from its very meager beginnings this store grew into one of the largest aquarium stores on the east Coast. He also owned a service company maintaining freshwater, saltwater and reef aquariums in homes and offices for over 28 years.

He has spent many years teaching and training his customers in the experts' way to keep fish, plants, invertebrates and corals healthy and thriving for years. Laurren's desire and passion is to share his accumulated knowledge, to help everyone become successful aquatic hobbyists. He is the aquarium expert at answers.com as well as creates informative educational products for the pet industry and aquarium hobbyist.

Consulting

For personal guidance over the phone or on-site consultation, Laurren can assist with installation of new aquarium or upgrades to existing aquariums. For all the details go to http://aquaticexperts.com/consulting/

Also on Amazon by Laurren Schmoyer:
Your New Saltwater Aquarium: A Step By Step Guide to Creating and Keeping a Stunning Saltwater Aquarium
Your New Freshwater Aquarium: A Step by Step Guide to Creating and Keeping a Stunning Freshwater Aquarium

This book has been published with the intent to provide accurate and authoritative information in regard to the subject matter within. While every precaution has been taken in preparation of this book, the publisher and author assume no responsibility for errors or omissions. Neither is any liability assumed for damages resulting from the use of the information herein.

Acknowledgements

I want to thank Eric and Scott Cohen of Sea Dwelling Creatures and Steven A. Dingeldein, MD for their species pictures, as well as David McLeod, D.D.S., for photos of his beautiful reef aquarium. I am grateful to Brandon Moon, owner of Elite Aquarium Services, for helping to ensure that the information is correct and useful. I am especially grateful for my wife, Elyse, and brother, Jeff, for their countless hours proofreading and their endless insight

Table of Contents

Preface 1
Introduction 2
   What is a Reef Aquarium? 2
Chapter 1 5
   Reef Basics Revealed 5
Chapter 2 9
   Components to Create a Living Reef 9
Chapter 3 61
   How to Assemble a Living Reef 61
Chapter 4 97
   Water Quality Explained 97
    The Nitrogen Cycle 99
Chapter 5 106
   How to Choose Fish for a Reef 106
   Bringing Your New Fish Home 134
   Methods to introducing fish to an aquarium: 136
Chapter 6 142
   Invertebrates are Beneficial and Fun 142
   Bringing Your New Invertebrates Home 174
Chapter 7 179
   Selecting and Placing Corals 179
   Bringing Your New Corals Home 213
Chapter 8 217
   How and What to Feed Fish, Invertebrates and Corals 217
Chapter 9 228
   Setting Up a Saltwater Quarantine Tank 228
   Eight Steps to Setting Up a Quarantine Tank 229

Chapter 10 235
  How to Care for a Reef...235
  15 Steps to Maintaining a Reef Aquarium 237
Appendix 250
  How to Cure Rock Taken From the Ocean 250
Glossary...252
More About the Author 254

Preface

Saltwater Reef aquariums when properly cared for are gorgeous, living slices of the ocean. The creatures they house are amazingly colorful, interesting and exotic! Reef keeping is an exciting hobby, and a strong foundation of saltwater knowledge ensures that your experience will be enjoyable and gratifying. With the right equipment and expert advice, keeping fish and corals healthy and thriving in an aquarium is fun. To help ensure your success, this manual will take you through a step-by-step process to assembling your reef aquarium. This guide will help you choose an aquarium, equipment, reef-safe fish, corals, invertebrates and so much more.

A living reef after one year

Introduction

What is a Reef Aquarium?

A reef aquarium is a saltwater aquarium that houses a collection of fish, corals, and invertebrates (i.e. crabs and shrimps) on and around a foundation of live rock (rocks with living organisms.) When assembled properly, a reef aquarium will be ecologically balanced and will mimic ocean reefs found throughout the world.

Oceans are filled with some truly amazing saltwater fish. Reef-safe or reef-compatible fish usually live well with corals and invertebrates. Regrettably, the majority of fish in the oceans eat corals and/or invertebrates. Fortunately, the ocean is huge and has an abundance of reef-safe fish with brilliant colors and unique personalities.

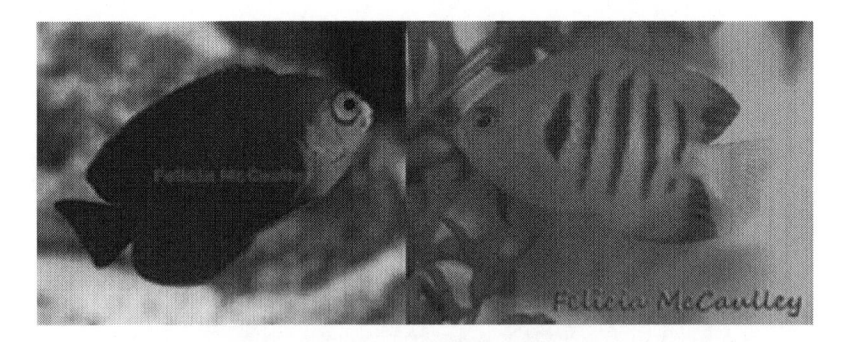

Pygmy and Flame Angelfish

While saltwater fish are magnificent alone in aquariums, imagine adding a collection of corals with their mind-blowing colors, shapes and breath-taking beauty.

Acanthastrea Lordhowensis Coral - a sample of its many colors

Green Hammer Coral

Live coral exists in every color and shape imaginable. Many hobbyists grow and propagate these gorgeous animals, and captive-raised corals are usually hardier, since they have not endured a stressful journey from the ocean.

Some invertebrates (i.e. crabs and snails) are beneficial to a reef because they consume algae growing on live rock, coral and sand. Invertebrates can also devour food left uneaten by fish.

Blood Red Fire Shrimp and Zebra Hermit Crab

There are also filter-feeding inverts that remove tiny bits of food from the water. Invertebrates are not only beneficial in a reef but some possess exotic beauty and most are amusing to watch.

Live rock is the foundation of our ocean reefs as well as our aquarium reefs. As its name may suggest, live rock is rock that has living organisms including (animals, plants, alga, bacteria, etc.) attached to and growing in and on it.

Fiji premium and Fiji shelf rock

We stack live rock in aquarium reefs to create caves, crevices and shelves, which, besides being aesthetically pleasing, give fish and invertebrates hiding places so that they can feel secure. Shelves are built into the rockwork at varying depths and are used to place corals.

You are about to start an amazing adventure. It is both a skill and an art to mix corals, invertebrates and fish from all over the world. This book will give you confidence and knowledge to create your own underwater masterpiece.

Chapter 1

Reef Basics Revealed

Before beginning to build a live reef aquarium there are a few items to consider. Reef aquariums are available in a range of sizes and can be set up using anything from very basic equipment, to highly advanced and technical equipment. Let us consider the difference the size of an aquarium has on a reef.

For the sake of definition in this book, we will consider an aquarium 'small' if it is less than 40 gallons; small reef aquariums are called ***Nano Reefs***. Large reef aquariums, also called ***Mini Reefs***, can be as large as 10,000 gallons or even more. The name may suggest that the reef is tiny, but compared to the natural reefs in the ocean, the name ***Mini Reef*** is actually appropriate.

Amazing Mini Reef with high-tech equipment

We will streamline our discussion to include only ***Mini Reefs***, not just because of their popularity, but also because of their obvious and not so obvious advantages. We will cover *Nano Reefs* in another volume.

Here are some benefits of a Mini Reef aquarium:
- Large aquariums are more stable than their smaller counterparts. Temperature and critical levels in large bodies of water will not fluctuate quickly.
- Large aquariums are more forgiving. If fish are overcrowded or overfed, there is more water to handle the mess.
- Many corals grow large and need constant trimming or they must be kept in a large aquarium.
- You can keep a larger variety of fish, invertebrates and corals.
- You can keep large-sized fish.
- You can keep more fish and/or schools of small fish.

As mentioned before, reef aquariums can be set up with anything from very basic equipment to the absolute extreme of high tech gadgets; or even some combination of low and high tech equipment. There are several reasons hobbyists use a mixed bag of equipment when setting up their reef aquarium:
- Many reef hobbyists begin as freshwater hobbyists and they often convert their existing aquariums into reefs. They may want to use some of the filtration they already own for the initial setup.
- Budget is another reason. Many hobbyists either cannot or do not want to spend a lot of money to build their reef.
- Some hobbyists purchase new or used equipment as they go along.
- Some just want to dip their toes in, starting with very basic equipment to see if they will enjoy the hobby before moving to a higher tech system.
- A few bold, courageous new hobbyists jump-in with both feet; they go for the extreme right from the very start!

The purpose of this guide is to help you choose the right equipment, whether you purchase one piece at a time or the entire system at once.

Starter or Basic Reef Setup

As mentioned earlier, many hobbyists convert freshwater aquariums to Mini Reefs and, depending on the long-term outlook, this idea can actually work quite well. Freshwater aquariums are generally standard aquariums (not drilled) so that all filtration equipment either works from inside or hangs on the back of the aquarium. There is a lot of reef equipment available for this type of setup, permitting hobbyists to create some attractive mini reefs with minimal financial investment.

The downside to this type of reef is that, when you look into the aquarium, you will see most of the equipment staring back at you. With all this equipment, it is difficult to create a breathtaking ocean reef scene to view the beautiful reef creatures.

Another challenge is that equipment hanging off the back of the aquarium can quickly becomes covered in salt or just plain dusty and dirty. These aquariums are normally set up in a living room and the filtration and other equipment can take away from the overall aesthetics of your creation.

The best way to keep equipment out of sight is to remove it from the aquarium. There are safe, aesthetically pleasing and effective ways to remove water from an aquarium, filter it, heat it, etc., and return it to the aquarium without flooding the floor. This is done through a single hole or series of holes drilled into an aquarium. A drilled aquarium with an overflow box will allow aesthetic advantages, while permitting versatility and the ability to create a beautiful piece of living furniture. Drilled aquariums are wonderful for reefs because all or most of the unsightly equipment can be installed externally from the aquarium; that way, all that you will see inside the aquarium is an amazing underwater reef scene.

In this book, we will discuss using a drilled aquarium with an overflow box because it creates versatility and permits us to assemble some of the most beautiful reefs on the planet.

> *TIP: Whether your budget allows you to get a top-of-the-line aquarium or you prefer to start with very basic equipment, the same principles apply across the board for water chemistry, water quality, keeping livestock, feeding, etc.*

Chapter 2

Components to Create a Living Reef

There are countless filters, pumps and other reef components readily available to construct a beautiful reef aquarium. We will be selecting equipment which fits below the aquarium in a cabinet, as opposed to that which hangs-on the aquarium. We will also discuss choosing and stacking live rock, and the importance of filtered freshwater not only to mix saltwater, but also to replace evaporated water.

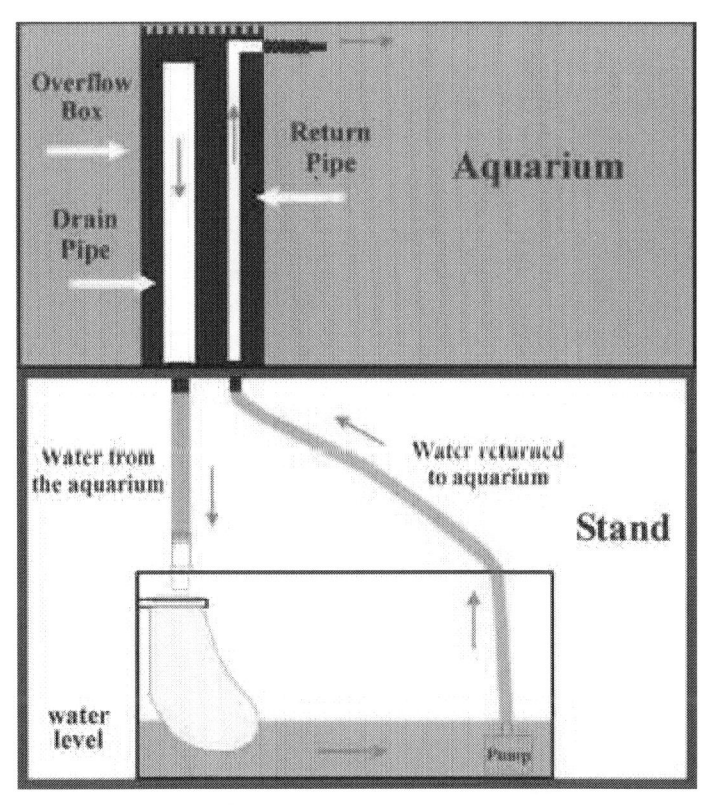

Diagram of a drilled aquarium with simple Berlin filter below in the stand

```
┌─────────────────────────────────────┐
│            Aquarium                 │
│                                     │
│    Overflow Box                     │
│         ────▶  ┌─────────┐         │
│                │  o   o  │         │
│                └──┼───┼──┘         │
└───────────────────┼───┼────────────┘
                   3/4"  1"
                  Return Drain
```

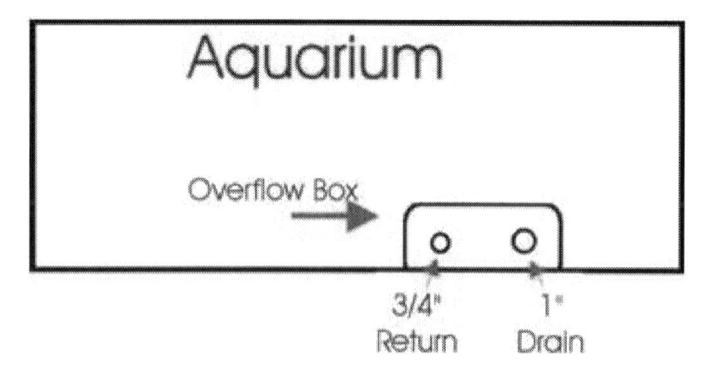

Drilled Aquariums with Overflows

A drilled aquarium is simply a standard aquarium with holes drilled in the back or bottom. These holes allow water to be removed from and returned to the aquarium. An overflow box is glued into the aquarium to surround the holes.

This illustration is a top view of two holes drilled in bottom of aquarium with an overflow box surrounding them.

Aquarium with overflow box (back view of aquarium)

Overflow boxes are generally made of glass, acrylic, or other food-grade plastic. An overflow box allows the water level in an aquarium to stay full or filled to a desired height. When the water evaporates from a non-drilled aquarium, the water level drops in the aquarium. When water evaporates in an aquarium with an overflow box, the water level in the filter drops and the aquarium always stays full. The key is the overflow box is built to a desired height to keep the aquarium full.

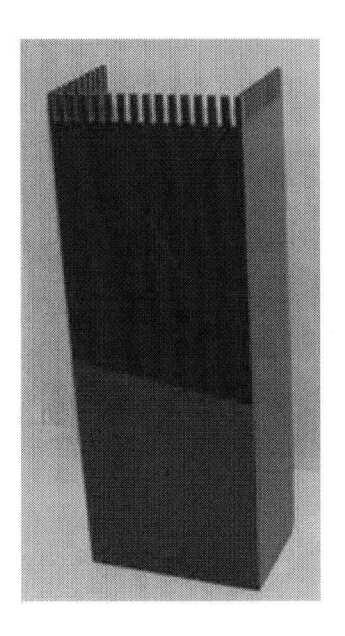

Overflow box with skimming teeth

As long as the water level in the aquarium reaches over the teeth (edge) of the overflow box, surface water will drop into the box, removing floating debris as well as a film that floats on the surface of aquarium water. Removing this film decreases the water's surface tension, allowing gases like carbon dioxide to escape while replenishing life-giving oxygen. This debris-free surface also allows more useable light to penetrate the surface; a plus for photosynthetic corals.

The slimy film removed with the overflow box is actually a combination of proteins, fats, and other organic and non-organic compounds. These compounds, skimmed off the surface of the aquarium water as they drop into the overflow box, travel through tubes through one of the holes drilled in the bottom of the aquarium and into a filter in the cabinet below. This is where the waste is removed.

How it works: A standard overflow box encases two holes drilled into the bottom of an aquarium. Attached to these two holes are two pieces of PVC pipe. The piece with the larger diameter is the drainpipe and the smaller diameter piece is the return. There are many styles of drain piping on the market and aquarists need only ensure that the chosen style is quiet.

Attached to the return pipe is a directional nozzle. This is used to return water back to the aquarium from the filter below.

There are many sizes and shapes of aquariums with overflow boxes already installed. If you already own a traditional aquarium, some fish stores can drill holes in your aquarium and install an overflow box as long as the aquarium glass is not tempered.

CAUTION: Tempered glass is often used in aquariums for its strength and because it is relatively lightweight. Before attempting to drill holes in an aquarium make certain that it does NOT have a tempered bottom. If someone tries to drill tempered glass it will shatter like the windshield of a car.

Next, we need bulkheads, pictured below. The one on the left is used for the return line and the one on the right is for the drain. Each has an O-ring (makes a seal to prevent leaks) and screw-on gasket.

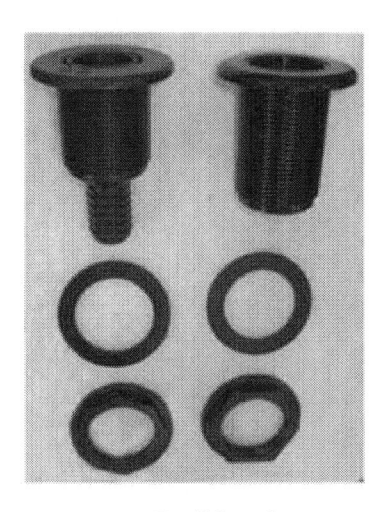

Bulkheads

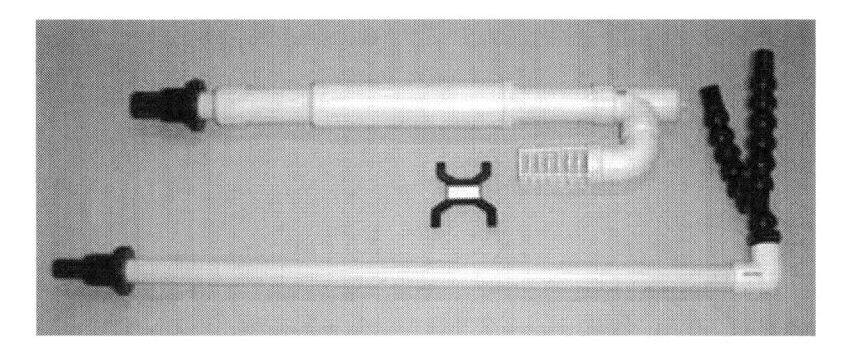

Drain and return assembly with directional nozzle

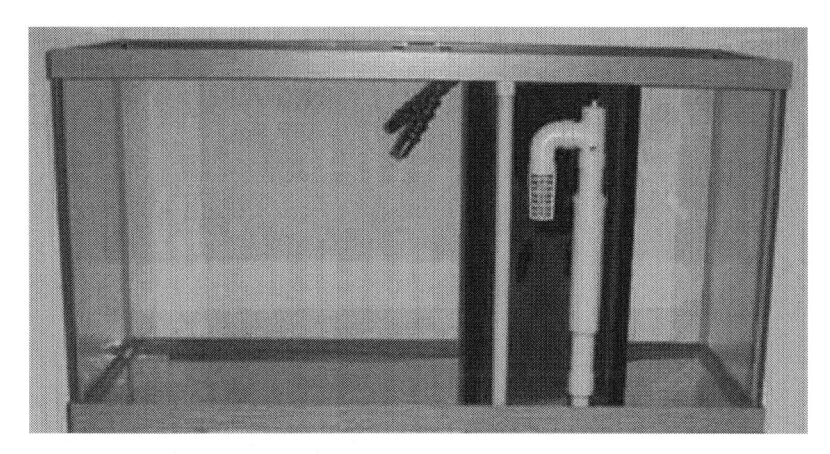

Drain and return assembly installed

Choosing a Mini Reef Aquarium

Different corals have different needs with regard to elevation, circulation, and lighting. When choosing a reef aquarium, the height, the width, and even the length are very important. Standard aquariums from 20 to 55 gallons are basically 12" from front glass to back glass. Stacking live rock in such a space will create an almost vertical rock wall that looks like a cliff. While the wall may look fine, there may be a shortage of ledges, on which to place corals so that they can receive plenty of light. Wider aquariums (at least 18 inches wide front to back) allow live rock stacking to easily create ledges and outcroppings on which to place live corals. Some ledges should be placed close to the top, others in high circulation areas, still others close to the bottom of the aquarium far from the light source. Keep in mind the benefits of a wide sandy area in front of the rockwork for bottom loving corals and some clams to live.

Shallow aquariums (from top to bottom) make it easier for cleaning and servicing, and allow more intense light for corals opposed to deep aquariums. As a general rule, the deeper the aquarium the larger and more expensive bulbs and lamp fixtures are required. Your best choice is to select an aquarium 12" to 30" deep.

The length of an aquarium can create the wow factor. When most people see an aquarium, at least 6 feet long in a home they say "WOW!" Another consideration when choosing a reef aquarium is to plan for the equipment to be plumbed into a cabinet below it. A larger cabinet makes it easier to house, plumb and service the necessary equipment. Most reef hobbyists choose an aquarium four to six feet in length.

Here are a few common reef aquarium sizes:

65 gallons - 36" (L) x 18" (W) x 24" (H)
90 gallons - 48" (L) x 18" (W) x 24" (H)
120 gallons - 48" (L) x 24" (W) x 24" (H)
180 gallons - 72" (L) x 24" (W) x 24" (H)
210 gallons - 72" (L) x 24" (W) x 29" (H)

The shapes of the above aquariums are all rectangles. You can create some beautiful reefs in aquariums shaped like cubes, cylinders, bow fronts - just about any shape you can imagine!

Lighting Explained

Reef lighting is one of the largest reef system equipment purchases; it dictates the types of corals that will live in the aquarium. Light brings out the beautiful unique colors and patterns of fish and many invertebrates.

Light is more than an aesthetic need. Most corals have symbiotic algae (zooxanthellae) living in their tissue which, through photosynthesis, create nutrients for the algae's coral host. In order for photosynthesis to take place, a specific spectrum of light is required. Our goal is to replicate this light in the reef aquarium.

There are several factors involved when choosing bulbs (lamps) and light fixtures. One must consider spectrum, intensity, budget, styles, and lamp types. Since there are so many different sizes, shapes and depths of aquariums, the method to determine the best lighting for your aquarium involves a bit of knowledge.

Light Bulb Ratings

Most reef aquarium light bulbs are rated in degrees of Kelvin (K), a numerical value attached to color emitted by a light source. For example, a lower value of around 5500 Kelvin is similar to sunlight gives off a yellow color. A light bulb with a higher Kelvin rating like 10000K gives off a crisp white light. Higher Kelvin ratings of 15000 to 20000K light bulbs give off blue to blue violet colors.

There is also one particular light bulb which radiates blue light with the popular name actinic. A "true" actinic bulb is not sold in degrees of Kelvin; it is manufactured to emit a specific wavelength (420 nm.) which is beneficial for corals.

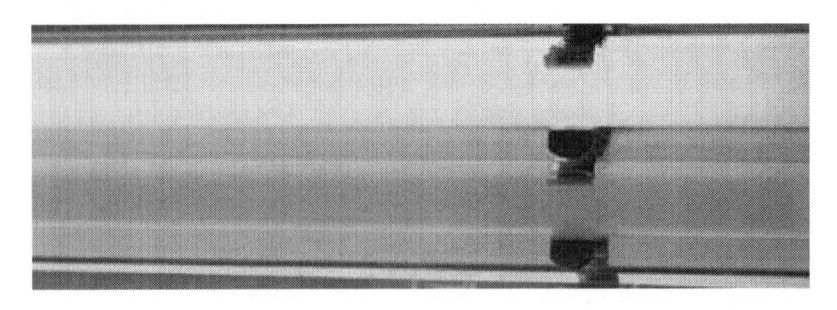

This picture shows black clips holding two fluorescent bulbs; the top lamp gives off white light and the lower lamp is actinic and gives off blue light

The depth a coral lives in the ocean helps reef aquarists determine the light requirements of that species. The further deeper the light penetrates ocean water, the more colors or wavelengths are filtered out, so corals living in water deeper than 50 feet "see" only blue and violet wavelengths. Aquarists have found that to achieve superior coral growth and good visual colors corals need full spectrum of light with extra blue. Most reef aquariums benefit from using 50% blue and 50% white light. For example, in a four-lamp fixture, use two 6500K light bulbs (full spectrum) and two actinic lamps. The 6500K is so bright that the blue will be indistinguishable. To achieve more of a blue hue use 10000K with actinic lamps. Either combination allows good coral growth. The closer to full spectrum the lamps, with the right intensity (discussed later) the faster our corals will grow.

Now that we understand the visual end we need to make sure our light penetrates deep enough into our aquariums to reach our corals.

Intensity

Choosing lamps which produce a pretty looking reef aquarium is the first part, but now we need to add some power (intensity.) To power lamps and send light into the water requires electricity (measured in watts.) For the most part, the higher the wattage of a light source the deeper the light will penetrate into the water. However, different manufacturers create products with differing results. So, depending on the lamp, ballast (power source to light the bulbs) and manufacturer we can get different amounts and types of light produced from the same Kelvin-rated bulbs. Because of this, pet and aquarium stores will recommend certain bulbs with certain ballasts to ensure consistent results. To guarantee you have enough intensity and usable light for photosynthesis, test lamps with a PAR meter (discussed shortly.)

Increasing wattage also means more electricity is required, resulting in higher power bills. One way to reduce this ongoing expense is to use high-polished metal reflectors. Fluorescent lamps give off 360 degrees of light. To make lamps more efficient, use a reflector to direct all the light into an aquarium. A reflector allows us to use a lower wattage lamp to achieve almost the same effect as a lamp with higher wattage.

PAR

We know photosynthesis takes place when photons are present at wavelengths between 400 and 700 nanometers. A PAR (Photosynthetically Active Radiation) meter can measure the light in a reef to ensure the proper wavelengths for corals at particular depths in the aquarium. Once we know the PAR value, we have a better idea of what types of corals to select as well as general placement in a reef aquarium. Since PAR meters have only been in use in the reef hobby in recent years, most books express coral lighting requirements in terms of low, medium or high light. An exact chart to convert lighting needs to PAR values is not available at this time. Some approximate PAR values are: low light will have PAR value of 50 to 120, medium light is 120 to 300 and high light is 300 and up.

The downside of checking PAR values is that PAR meters are fairly expensive, but some aquarium stores have them to lease for short periods of time. If using a PAR meter is not an option, research each coral's particular lighting requirement (recommended coral books in back of this guide) and place corals in your reef with your best educated guess. If a coral thrives in its location, great; if not, move it towards or away from the light source. The PAR value is highest at the top of your aquarium and can drop considerably in lower regions, depending on the lighting system.

Many manufacturers state the PAR values at different depths for their light fixtures. If the PAR value is unknown, ask you dealer for suggestions.

Light Bulbs Types

Fluorescent and Compact Fluorescent

Fluorescent bulbs (lamps) including T8-size Standard High Output (HO), Very High Output (VHO) and Compact Fluorescent (also known as power compact) light systems were a popular choice in the past but have been massively replaced by more efficient T5 High Output Fluorescent lamps.

Compact Fluorescents and VHO's are still available and produce a bright intense light, which will grow many corals and anemones. These intense lamps produce much heat, and it is necessary to use a fan to keep this heat from transferring into your aquarium water raising its temperature. T8 lamps are also fairly expensive to replace.

In comparison, T5 fluorescent lamps use less electricity than their T8 predecessors. Also, T5 lamps can produce a light almost twice as bright as a standard florescent lamp. Combining a new improved mirror reflector with a T5 bulb puts out about the same amount of PAR value as the older intense lights with a lower electric bill and less heat.

T5 fluorescent lamps with reflectors

Another benefit of T5 compared to the old fluorescent lamps is they are physically smaller only 5/8" in diameter, allowing more light, with less space.

T5 fluorescent lights work great in aquariums less than 20" deep for keeping low and medium light corals and sea anemone. It is possible to grow SPS corals in very shallow aquariums with T5 bulbs. A PAR meter will tell you for sure.

When housing photosynthetic corals and other photosynthetic inverts it is best to replace the fluorescent bulbs every year.

Metal Halide

Metal halide lighting has been time-tested and proven to grow light needy Small Polyp Stony (SPS) Corals and Tridacna Clams or for a deep reef aquarium. Metal halide lamps produce an intense beam of light and create a beautiful shimmering effect inside the aquarium.

Metal halide aquarium lights have two different styles of sockets: single and double ended called HQI bulbs. Both style bulbs are effective at keeping all types of corals. As with their fluorescent counterparts, it is beneficial to use reflectors that are special made for halide bulbs. These reflectors (pictured below) will channel the rays' of light emitted into the water, enabling the use of lower wattage light bulbs, as well as saving money on the electric bill.

T5 bulbs with reflectors and metal halide reflectors (halide bulbs not shown)

Most hobbyists use fluorescent fixtures with T5 lamps (actinic blue bulbs - 420 nm) in tandem with metal halide lights to create a sun up to sun down effect; automatic light timers are used to turn on T5 lamps alone for an hour or two; then halide lights turn on later. Halides run for six to ten hours, turning off an hour or two before the T5s.

Metal halide lamps create intense heat. These bulbs need to be cooled with fans and the bulbs must be at least six inches from the surface of the aquarium water. Sometimes a chiller is necessary to keep the aquarium water temperature from heating up. For the lamps to produce this very intense light, they also use a lot of electricity. Metal halide bulbs are available from 150 to 1000 watts.

Metal halide bulbs need to be replaced every 6 to 12 months. A PAR meter can be used to test the bulbs and tell you exactly when they need to be replaced for your particular livestock.

LED

The newest light to hit the reef market is the LED. Their versatility makes them the future of aquarium lighting. LED bulbs have created massive excitement with many manufacturers competing to create the best state-of-the-art reef lighting systems. LED lights have some impressive qualifications.

Energy Efficient

Metal halides produce light using electricity to heat a filament until it becomes very hot; as a result, a metal halide bulb will radiate most of its energy as heat, not light. An LED bulb is much more efficient at converting electricity to light while it emitting a fraction of the heat of a halide. The heat produced by LED lights and electrical components are also pulled away from the aquarium water into the air by a heat sink (a passive device that absorbs and dissipates heat). Fans may also be used to cool a fixture and blow heat away for the aquarium. Because very little heat is transferred to the aquarium water, the need for a chiller may be eliminated.

Long Lasting

LED bulbs are energy efficient. This means less power consumption resulting in a lower electric bill. In addition, manufacturers claim that LED bulbs can provide optimum light output for 50,000 hours! That means you would have over ten years before LED bulbs need to be replaced. Many other types of reef lamps need to be replaced every six months to a year.

LED white and blue bulbs with reflector around each bulb

Plenty of PAR

There are many LED fixtures which boast impressive PAR values that provide enough light to easily grow light-needy Small Polyp Stony (SPS) Corals. Some light systems far exceed what corals require and can bleach or burn corals. To solve this problem, most fixtures have a controller to reduce the intensity. It is best to choose a fixture that produces too much light so you can set it to your corals desired light requirements.

Total Control

Most LED fixtures come with different color LED bulbs and use a controller to customize the color to personal preference. Choose a comfortable color on your eyes that will also give optimum coral growth. A benefit many controllers have is that they mimic Mother Nature with sunrise to sunset, cloud movement, moon phases, and a host of other features.

Shimmering Light

LED lights create a shimmering effect similar to metal halide bulbs as they imitate lights seen on the ocean. The shimmering is altered by distance the light bulbs are above the aquarium as well as water and air movement.

At this time, LED lighting fixtures are uniquely made by each manufacturer. It is best to choose a manufacturer you trust and go with their recommendations. Some LED fixtures are architectural beauties with a modern profile and sleek look. With the huge selection of LED lighting available there is one that is ideal for your aquarium.

Moonlight LEDs

Reef aquariums are very active at nighttime. To view a reef at night without disturbing its inhabitants, place a light fixture over the aquarium with one or several blue LEDs. After the main aquarium lights go off at night, these few blue LEDs generate a beautiful, blue shimmering light, adding a calming and even majestic ambiance. These blue LEDs, when turned on at nighttime are called moonlights and will make some corals fluoresce, creating a stunning effect.

36" LED fixture with two moonlight bulbs

Moonlight in the oceans influences feeding and spawning behavior. It is still undetermined whether LEDs can cause the same effect as the moon. We do know that using blue LEDs on an established reef tank late at night is a wonder to behold.

Light Fixtures Come in a Variety of Styles

Aquarium light fixtures come in a variety of different shapes and styles; this makes it easy to find one to suit your needs. These fixtures can mount on top of an aquarium, hang above it, or even attach to the inside of a canopy. Which fixture is right for you is determined by your personal preference and the look of your aquarium. Do you want to see your lighting fixture or do you prefer to have it hidden behind a wall or enclosed in a canopy?

Mount Directly On an Aquarium

Some light fixtures are specifically designed to sit either directly on top of the glass top on the aquarium, or may use 'legs' to lift the fixture. Legs or frame mounts are usually adjustable to ensure that the light fixture will fit different manufacturers' aquariums with similar lengths. Frame mounts are made to hold the fixture securely in place, keeping it from accidently being knocked into an open aquarium. Frame mounts raise the light fixture making it easier to work inside the aquarium.

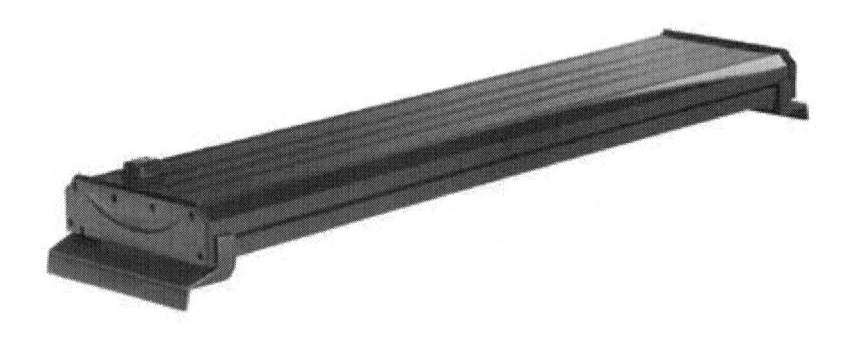

LED light fixture with adjustable mounting legs by Aqueon

Hanging Light Fixture

Many fixtures come with hanging kits to suspend the fixtures above the aquarium. These kits still require a wall or hanging plant bracket, or decorative ceiling hooks to hang the light fixture above an aquarium.

If you do not want to hang your light from a wall or ceiling, try a light fixture hanger which has one or two suspension arms that attach to a wide variety of aquarium stands or furniture. The adjustable arms extend over the aquarium making it easy to suspend your light fixture.

Some fixtures have flexible gooseneck which one side attaches to the aquarium and the other to the fixture. The goosed neck flexible arm allows it to position the light in the ideal location about your aquarium

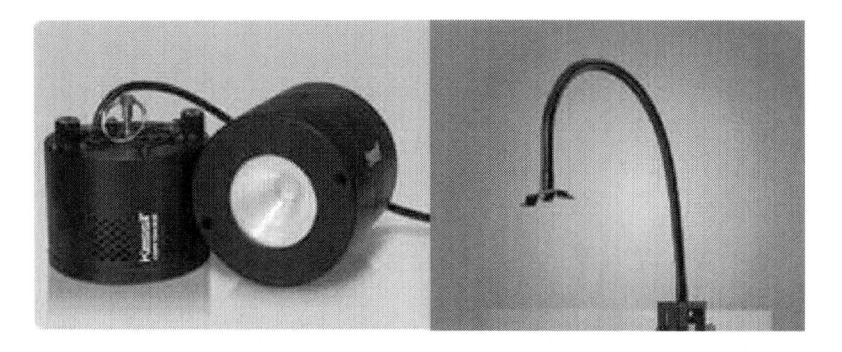

Kessils' LED lights Pendant can hang or attach to flexible gooseneck with aquarium mounting bracket

Mount In a Canopy

To make an aquarium look more like a piece of furniture, many hobbyists use decorative stands and add a matching canopy to the top of the tank. Canopies are generally made of wood or plastic and enclose the top of the aquarium concealing the top rim, light fixture and other equipment. The inside of a canopy is typically constructed so that a light fixture can easily be mounted. Attaching a light fixture to the inside of a canopy allows ample space for the hobbyist to feed the fish and care for the aquarium. There are a variety of mountable lights which include either mounting brackets or stainless steel screws to mount the fixture directly to the canopy. Small pendant lights, such as those manufactured by Kessill, include a hanging bolt making them a breeze to install.

TIP: Once you choose a lighting system go to YouTube and watch a video and see how looks when it is installed and if it is appeals to you.

Lighting Thoughts and Examples

Soft corals such as Mushrooms, Leather and Zoanthids do not require intense (bright) light to thrive. Large Polyp Stony (LPS) Corals such as Frogspawn, Bubble, Cup, Torch and Hammer corals need much more intense light than Soft Corals. Small Polyp Stony (SPS) Corals such as Acropora, Pocillipora and Montipora require very intense light to thrive. (Generally in the same aquarium SPS Corals should be placed closer to the light than LPS Corals, and Soft Corals should be farthest from the light.) If you plan to keep only Soft Corals you are safe with a less expensive, lower wattage system. Acroporas, however, require intense light, and a larger budget.

Consider the types of corals and photosynthetic invertebrates (discussed in Selecting and Placing Corals and Invertebrates are Beneficial and Fun) that you would like to keep in your reef before choosing a lighting system. Also, it is wise to take into consideration the heat generated by the lighting system and the operating costs when weighing the prices of the different systems.

Here are a few reef lighting examples using T5's and metal halides:

Low Light
75 gallon reef (48"Lx18"Wx20"H) with Soft Corals and Sea Anemones
    1 - Four lamp T5 light fixture with reflectors
    2 - T5 HO 48" 54 watt light bulbs - Actinic
    2 - T5 HO 48" 54 watt light bulbs - 10000K

Medium Light
90 gallon reef (48"Lx18"Wx24"H) with Soft Corals and LPS Corals
    1 - Light fixture with 2 x 175 watt metal halide and 2 x T5's with reflectors
    2 - 175 watt metal halide bulb - 1500K
    2 - T5 HO 48" 54 watt light bulbs - Actinic

High Light
120 gallon reef (48"Lx24"Wx24"H) with LPS and SPS Corals

1 - Light fixture with 2 x 250 watt metal halide and four T5's with reflectors

2 - 250 watt metal halide bulb - 1500K

4 - T5 HO 48" 54 watt light bulbs - Actinic

Berlin Filters

A Berlin filter has a sump or water holding chamber with a mechanical filter and space for a protein skimmer and other equipment. It is usually placed below the aquarium and preferably in a cabinet stand. Berlin filter can be very basic or may be extremely deluxe with lots of compartments and built in refugium walls.

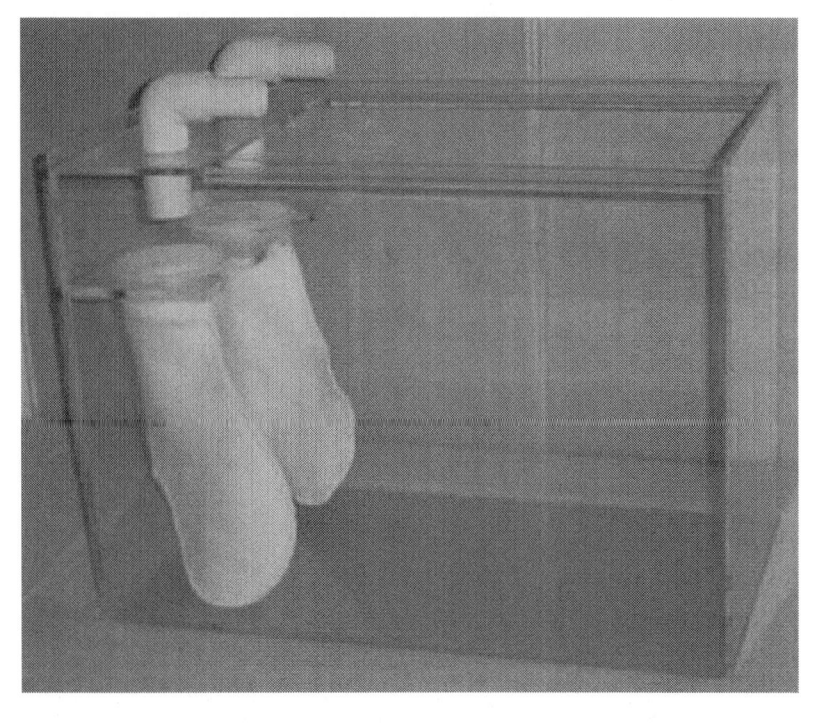

Basic - Berlin sump with two sock hangers and filter socks

Deluxe - sump has two sock hangers, refugium compartment, protein skimmer and return water pump compartment

A Berlin filter is placed below the aquarium, usually in a cabinet stand. Water is routed from the overflow box of the aquarium through a drain line down to the Berlin filter. This water then flows through a pre-filter and collects in the bottom of the filter.

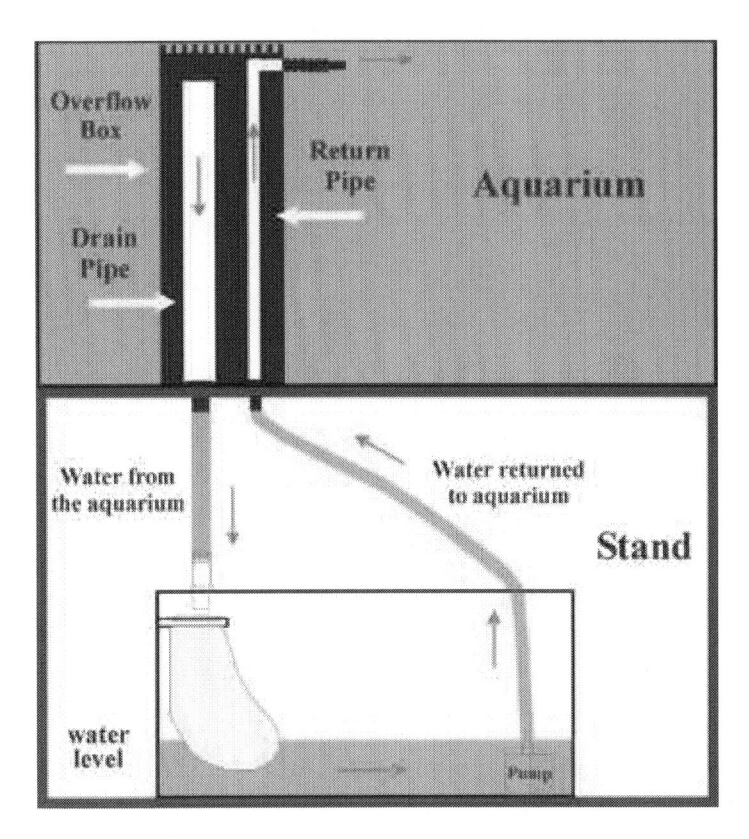

Diagram shows placement of Berlin filter and water flow

    The pre-filter can be a sheet of fiber material in a tray or a filter bag or sock, as pictured. The purpose of the pre-filter is to physically or mechanically remove large particles from the water. The sock(s) and other pre-filter materials should be cleaned and/or replaced often. The amount of livestock will dictate how often the media must be cleaned or changed.

    As a filter sock gets dirty, the water inside the sock rises until it eventually flows over the top of the sock. All physical filtration media will eventually clog with debris and must be replaced. The more often you clean your media, the better the water quality of your aquarium. A dirty mechanical filter will eventually lead to increased nitrates as bacteria grow in the media to process the accumulated waste. Hence, it is important to replace physical filtration media often.

After solid debris is removed from aquarium water by the pre-filter, the water can be processed through a protein skimmer, one of the main keys to filtration in a Berlin system.

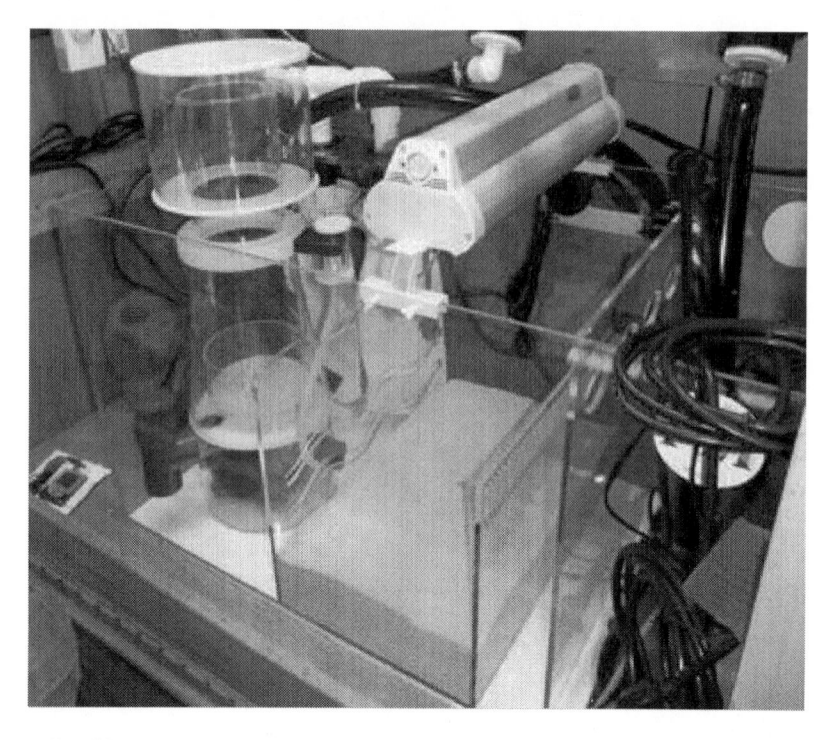

Berlin filter, protein skimmer and refugium compartment in center with white sand

The Berlin filter also holds the return pump and heater, which allows the display tank to be free of the clutter of necessary aquarium equipment.

Protein Skimmers

Have you ever noticed the foam left when waves crash on the shore as you stroll along the beach?

Waves crashing on the beach leave protein foam and other wastes behind

    This foam is composed of protein and wastes from the ocean. Protein skimmers attempt to mimic the action caused by these aerated, crashing waves.

    Protein skimmers physically remove dissolved organic compounds and other substances from aquarium water. These organic compounds are a product of uneaten fish foods, fish waste, dead plants, bacteria and decomposing matter. Organic compounds in the water break down into several by-products, one of which is ammonia.

    High levels of ammonia are toxic to fish and invertebrates. Biological filtration reduces ammonia to a final product called nitrates. Natural seawater is continuously moving, and reef areas where high levels of nitrates are produced are constantly being replenished with low-nitrate water from the ocean depths. In a closed system like an aquarium levels of nitrate can quickly rise to toxic levels.

    Protein skimmers remove wastes before they are broken down into nitrates. That means higher water quality for aquarium inhabitants.

Example of internal protein skimmer

Internal protein skimmer in Berlin sump

How Does A Skimmer Work?

There are many types and designs of protein skimmers. Most skimmers have some basic components in common. They consist of a vertical chamber filled by a pump where water is mixed with fine bubbles. Dissolved organic compounds are attracted to the surface of the bubbles within the skimmer and join themselves to the bubbles as they rise.

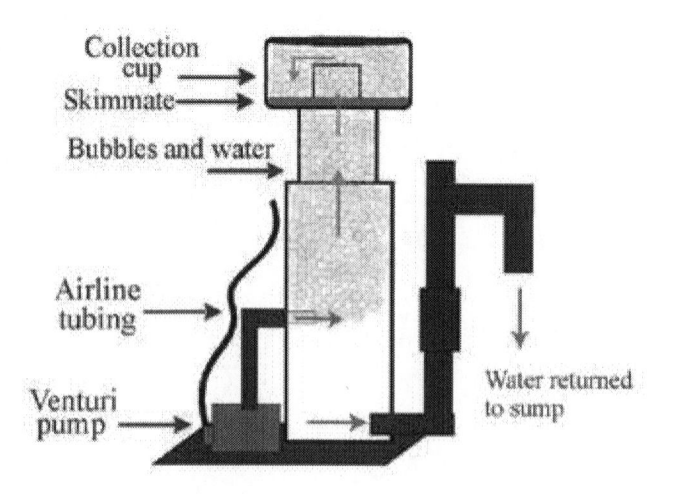

In-sump protein skimmer - Follow the arrows to see the flow of water (green arrows), bubbles and waste (orange arrows)

As these bubbles rise to the top of the chamber they produce foam. This foam is the same foam you see washed up on shore at the beach. As the foam rises up the chamber it falls into a collection cup. The bubbles pop and the compounds are collected in a cup and removed from the aquarium water. The product that is collected in the cup is referred to as skimmate. The collection cup is emptied periodically to remove these wastes from the system.

There are four general configurations of protein skimmers: internal protein, hang-on aquarium, in-sump and freestanding skimmers. In each of these categories, you will find many designs.

TIP: A skimmer that is too small will not operate effectively and will require more maintenance than one that is sized correctly for the gallons in the reef. Skimmer sizing on retail packaging can be rather general, and it may be prudent to purchase a skimmer that is rated for a larger aquarium.

Choosing a Quality Protein Skimmer

Here is what you need to know when choosing a protein skimmer.

The size of the bubble is very important. If the bubble is large, it will rise to the surface quickly. Smaller bubbles rise more slowly in the water column than larger bubbles, giving more time for organic compounds to attach to them. Small bubbles also have more surface area than large bubbles (in the same size skimmer) providing more surface area to which organic compounds can attach.

The water column in your protein skimmer should be almost white with bubbles. This means there will be millions of bubbles in the water column. If there is a lot of water with just a few bubbles, the skimmer will not efficiently remove organic compounds.

An efficient protein skimmer will have thick, dark-colored waste in its collection cup. If the waste is watery and pale greenish or yellow in color adjust the water level or bubble size.

The waste collection cup should be easy to remove for cleaning.

This protein skimmer sits inside a Berlin sump. Note the white column of fine bubbles

Protein skimmers require periodic cleaning to keep them running efficiently. When choosing a protein skimmer, be sure the parts that need cleaning are easily accessible and removable.

Water Pumps and Power Heads

Water Pumps
Overflow boxes skim water off the surface of an aquarium and channel water down to a wet/dry or Berlin filter. A pump then returns the water to your aquarium.

The pump can be internal (placed inside the Berlin filter) or external (outside the Berlin filter.) Choose a pump designed to handle saltwater.

Internal Water Pumps

Internal water pumps come in an assortment of sizes based on how many gallons per hour it pumps. It generally cost less than external pumps.

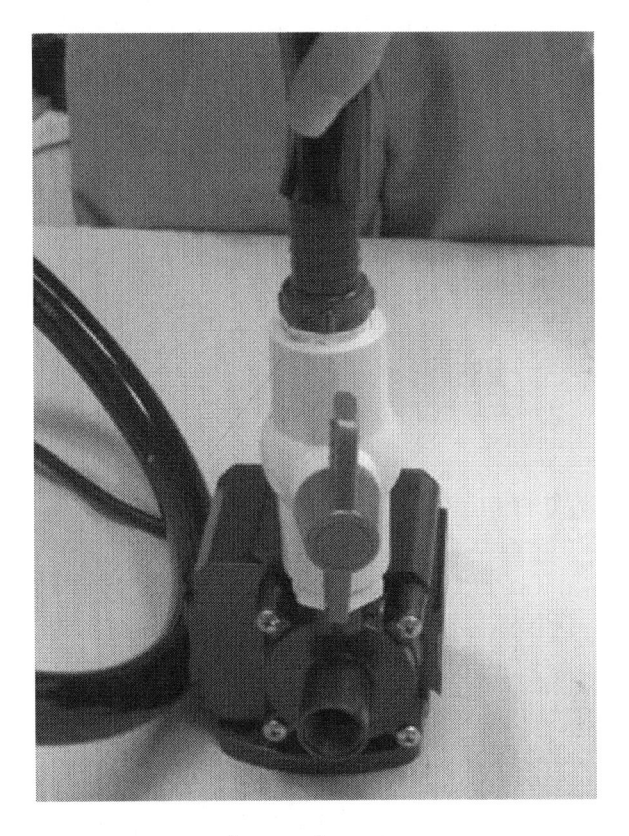

Internal pump

Advantages of Internal Water Pumps
- Easy to install and replace.
- If the pump or fittings to the pump ever leak water drains back into the filter.
- Pumps are usually very quiet.
- Generally compact in size.

Internal return pump in back of last chamber on right, highlighted by lime outline. Front internal pump in right chamber goes to chiller

External Water Pumps

Most external water pumps have a cooling fan built in to remove the heat the pump generates. This means less heat is transferred directly to the aquarium water. These water pumps come in an assortment of sizes based on how many gallons per hour it pumps. External water pumps need a hole cut into the filter with piping to channel the water outside the filter to the pump.

External water pump

Advantages of External Water Pumps
- Available in larger sizes for big aquariums.
- Leaves room inside the Berlin filter for other equipment.
- Very little heat is transferred to the aquarium water.
- Noisy water pumps can be plumbed at a location away from the aquarium.

External pump plumbed into a Berlin filter

Choosing the Right Size Water Pump

Ideally, you want to turn your aquarium water over between three to five times each hour through your sump. Therefore, if you have a 90-gallon aquarium you need to have a pump that can pump 270 to 450 gallons each hour.

Another important factor in selecting a pump is "head pressure". Head pressure is determined by how high the pump is returning water to your aquarium. If the water pump is located under your aquarium and it has to push water back over the side of the aquarium we would measure that the height (in feet) of the side of the aquarium to determine the head pressure.

If we measure the height from the pump to the aquarium rim and it is at four feet than we have four feet of head pressure.

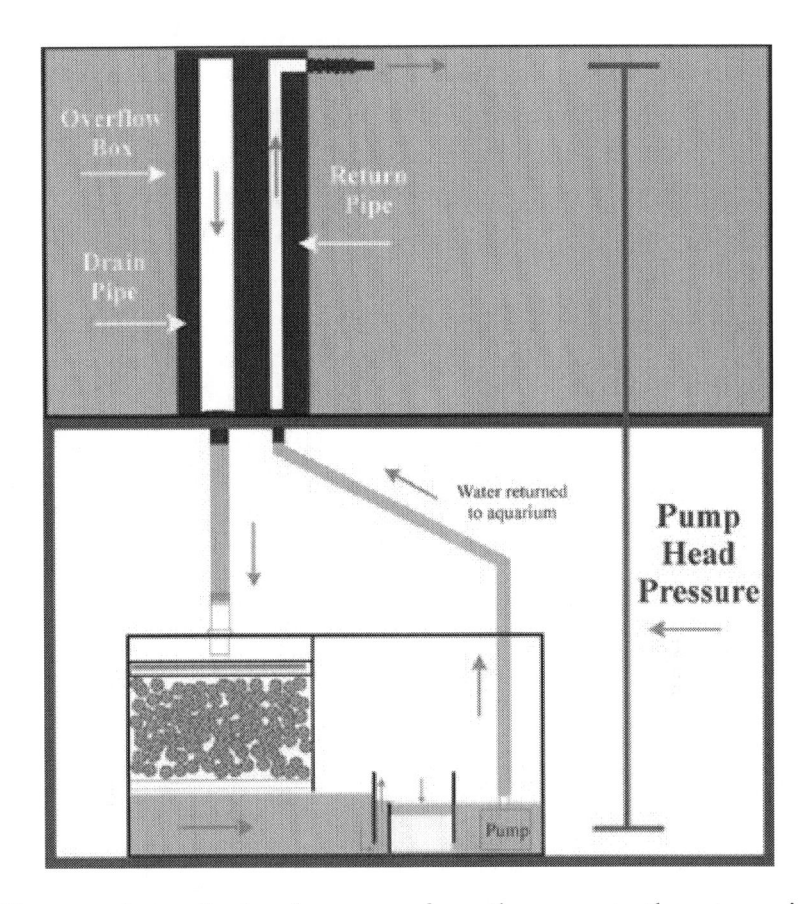

Diagram shows the head pressure from the pump to the return pipe

Each water pump manufacturer has a chart showing the number of gallons the pump pushes at different head pressures. Once you determine the amount of water (in gallons) you want your aquarium to turn over in a given hour use the chart to choose the correct size pump for your aquarium.

Powerheads

A powerhead is a small submersible water pump. They have many uses including:
- Circulation of water inside your aquarium.
- Pumping water through protein skimmers, UV sterilizers, reactors and other equipment.

Powerheads are ideal for additional circulation inside your aquarium. Many times there are areas of low flow within an aquarium. Mounting a small powerhead with its nozzle pointing in the direction where extra flow is needed will ensure you have water movement throughout your aquarium.

Examples of powerheads

Just like water pumps, powerheads are rated by the number of gallons per hour of water they pump. It is important that the flow rate of the powerhead is suitable to the particular application for which it is intended. Check the chart that comes with the particular brand and model you want to use.

Powerheads are available in a nozzle or wide flow style. Powerheads with a nozzle output (which produce a straight, or linear, high pressure flow) are easy to attach to tubing used in conjunction with protein skimmers, UV sterilizers, and other equipment. They are also useful in situations where the aquarist needs flow directed in a specific area in the aquarium.

Powerheads with a wide flow output (called diffuse flow) are useful in creating general flow throughout the aquarium. These powerheads are commonly used in tanks with live rock to ensure flow throughout the water column in the tank. These pumps also move a high water volume at a low pressure, creating a wide, gentle flow when compared to the constricted jet of water created by nozzle-output powerheads. This wider flow at low pressure is especially essential in reef tanks, assuring filter feeding invertebrates have access to suspended food particles in the aquarium water.

When used within an aquarium, a powerhead can be attached with a hanger, suction cups, or magnets. Over time suction cups stiffen and lose their grip on the aquarium glass. The hanger style limits where you can place your powerhead in your aquarium to an area within several inches of the tank's rim. The best choice is a magnetic clip-on style. Magnets make for easy placement anywhere on the glass of your aquarium and won't give out over time.

Wavemaker

Wavemakers create random current throughout the aquarium. Most aquariums have spots of no or low water flow areas around corals or live rock where waste accumulates. A wave like action and random currents will send the waste up into the water column where it can be removed by mechanical filtration.

There are many different types and styles of wavemakers, but we will focus on the ones which control multiple water pumps and powerheads. Normally water pumps and powerheads create a constant stream of water. Once their power cords are plugged into a wavemaker they can now create random currents. The wave maker can turn water pumps or powerheads on and off and some can even increase or decrease the flow rate. Wavemakers can range from inexpensive to very expensive.

Example of a wavemaker controller

The low end models are basically timers that turn your powerheads on and off every 15 to 90 seconds. The more expensive models have buttons you push to change the different types of wave patterns. Some will include a button to push for feeding that turns the powerheads off or down and leaves the main water pump running. This period of time allows the fish to eat without its food being blown around the aquarium. Some have night cycles which reduce the water currents.

Refugium

Because of its many benefits to a saltwater or reef aquarium a refugium makes a great addition. Like inlets and saltwater marshes, modern refugiums house microorganisms and macro algae nestled on a deep sand and/or mud bed with live rock. A refugium can be as simple as a glass aquarium or an acrylic box with chambers created by partitions or baffles, with a light placed above it.

Refugiums provide many benefits to the main or display aquarium. Macro algae, mud and/or sand become natural filters for reducing nitrates, silicates, and phosphates. Reducing excess organic nutrients helps control unwanted algae growth in the display aquarium. Also, the refugium lights are set to turn on at times opposite the display aquarium, stabilizing oxygen and pH levels.

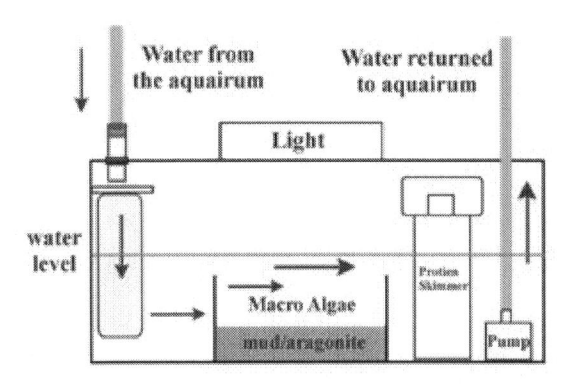

Pictured is a refugium with deep substrate and thick plant life

Since the refugium is generally separate from the main aquarium, it provides protection for copepods and amphipods (sold at most aquarium stores) giving your aquarium a constant, natural food source. This natural food can be netted from the refugium or will travel naturally to the display aquarium via the lines connecting the two. To keep this natural food source, never put predators such as fish, shrimp, and corals in your refugium.

Refugium Styles
Refugiums come in a variety of styles including hang-on, internal, stand-alone and built-in.

A **hang-on refugium** consists of an acrylic box with baffles, a small submersible water pump to pump water from the aquarium into the refugium, and a light. The water flows through the refugium and gravity feeds it back to the aquarium. Just add mud or sand and macro algae and it is ready to go.

An **internal refugium** is built inside the main aquarium with sections of the aquarium divided off.

A **stand-alone refugium** is housed in an aquarium outside the display aquarium. This style refugium uses an aquarium with dividers or baffles, a pump and a return system. The stand-alone refugium can be attached above, beside or below your display aquarium. Depending on the location of the refugium the water is either pumped or gravity fed back to the main aquarium.

A **built-in refugium** is built into a trickle filter or Berlin sump. Water is normally gravity fed from the main aquarium through pre-filtered media (to remove large debris) then through the refugium. A series of glass or acrylic walls allow water to pass through the refugium section, keeping mud and algae from passing through the return-line to the display aquarium. These walls also slow water flow to assist with macro algae feeding.

Built-in-refugium with sand, macro algae and light

The size refugium needed, depends on the bio-load of the display aquarium. A larger refugium is necessary for a heavily stocked display aquarium, a smaller refugium may be used for a lightly stocked aquarium.

Once a refugium style is chosen and it is plumbed to the display aquarium and is ready to set up. Add a commercial refugium mud and/or an oolithic (sugar size) aragonite sand to a depth of up to six inches; add live rock and macro algae.

Macro Algae

Chaetomorpha, Ulva (Sea Lettuce), halimeda (red seaweed) and Gracilaria (red seaweed) are macro algae that do well in refugiums. These macro algae remove nitrates and phosphates from aquarium water. Regular trimming and thinning of these plants also removes phosphates and nitrates from the system.

Lighting

Place a light over the refugium to grow macro algae. The bulb should be 5,000 to 6,500 Kelvin for optimum plant growth. Choose a light fixture that produces at least 4 watts per gallon of water in the refugium (for those less than 16 inches deep.)

TIP: Use an appliance timer and set the refugium light to turn on when the display light goes out.

During the day, when exposed to light, plants and algae in the display aquarium use up carbon dioxide and give off oxygen. When the display aquarium light is off photosynthesis no longer takes place and CO2 levels rise. Carbon dioxide (CO_2) is an acid, so pH lowers at night when the light is out.

With a refugium light on while the display aquarium lights are off, plants in the refugium will use CO_2 and produce oxygen keeping the pH in the entire system stable. This ensures the nighttime oxygen levels do not drop as sharply as in a reef without a refugium

Ultra Violet Sterilizers (optional)

A UV Sterilizer (UV for short) uses an ultraviolet light to kill single-celled organisms such as bacteria, viruses, protozoan, and algae cells that are floating in water which passes past the UV bulb.

A UV consists of a plastic or stainless steel housing through which water is pumped around and past a germicidal bulb. It is best to use a UV that uses a quartz sleeve between the bulb and the water. The quartz sleeve makes it easier to change the bulb.

These units come in two styles: Hang-on or in-line. Water is pumped through the sterilizer using a powerhead, a canister filter, or an internal or external water pump.

Ultraviolet light has a wavelength between 250 and 280 nm which kills organisms by altering their DNA at the cellular level. UV units are effective in eliminating most disease-causing organisms and when used properly, go a long way towards keeping a healthy aquarium.

There are several factors that influence the efficiency of a UV sterilizer:
- Contact time between water and UV bulb (dwell time)
- Clarity of water
- Age of bulb
- Intensity or wattage of bulb

The contact time between the water and the bulb is critical - if the water's flow rate is too fast, contact time with the UV light is reduced so that the sterilizer is ineffective. The flow rate should be slow enough to maximize the time water spends within the UV's housing (check manufacturer's recommended flow rate for your particular model.)

The clarity of the water being sterilized is another factor influencing the efficiency of the unit. Ultraviolet sterilizers are typically placed in-line after water leaves the filter for this reason. The cleaner the water, the more efficient the sterilizer will be.

The age of the UV bulb directly relates to the effectiveness of a UV sterilizer. The sterilization impact of the UV drops considerably after about six months to one year of use (depending on the unit.) The bulb will still light up, but the spectrum of the lamp will have shifted and it is no longer as effective at killing free-floating organisms.

UV sterilizer are designed to hang on the back of an aquarium or plumbed-in-line between your filter's return pump and your aquarium. This ensures that 100 percent of the water that passes through the sump also goes through the UV. Make sure the UV sterilizer and the return pump are the proper size for your aquarium.

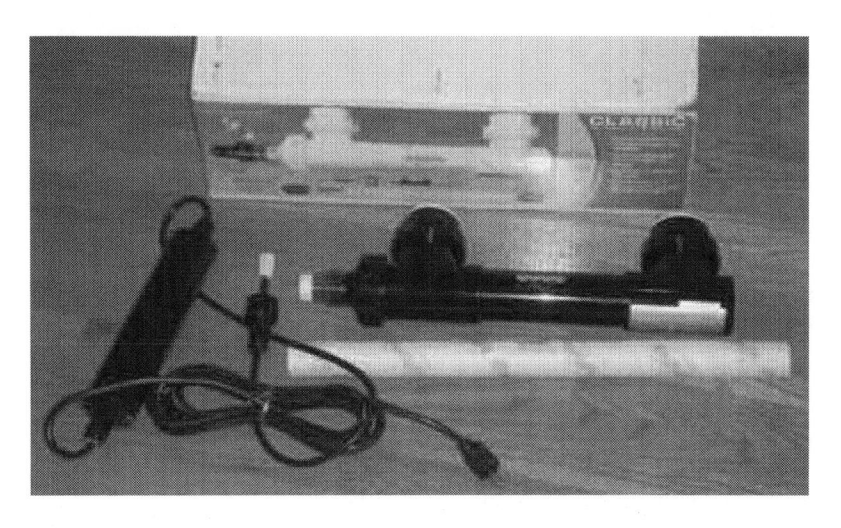

40 watt inline UV sterilizer

Another way to plumb an inline UV sterilizer into your aquarium is to drop a smaller water pump into your sump and push the water through the sterilizer and return it back to the sump. This is easy to install but does not allow for 100 percent of the water to pass through the sterilizer. Again to be most effective have all the water returning to the aquarium pass through the correct size UV sterilizer.

CAUTION: Never look at a UV bulb while it is on. UV light will severely damage the retina. The UV bulb is shielded inside of housing for your protection.

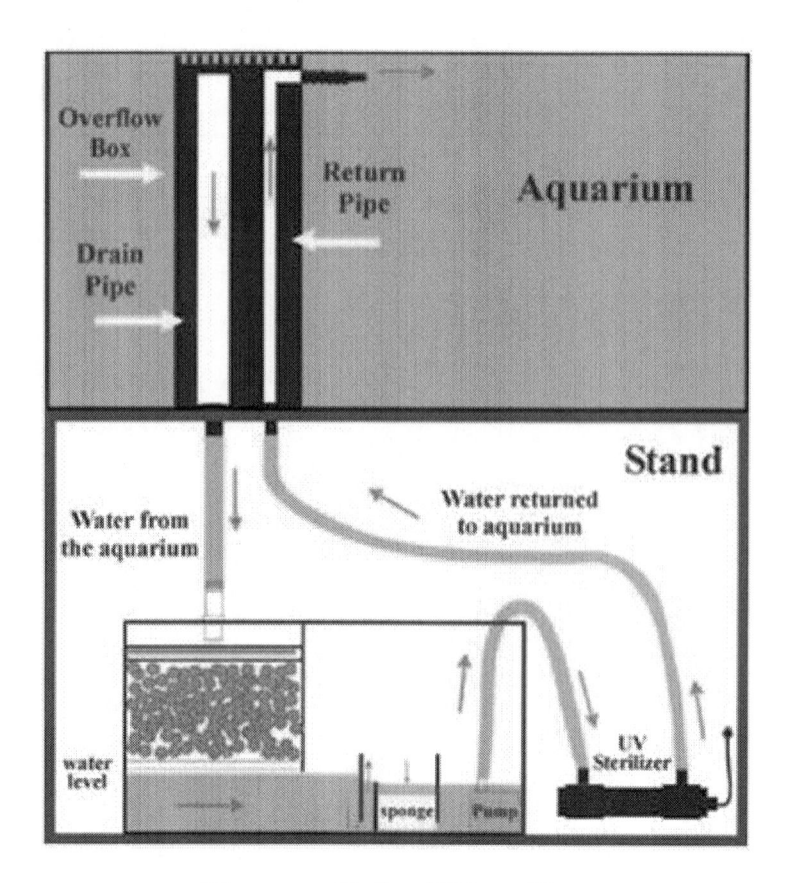

Diagram of inline UV sterilizer

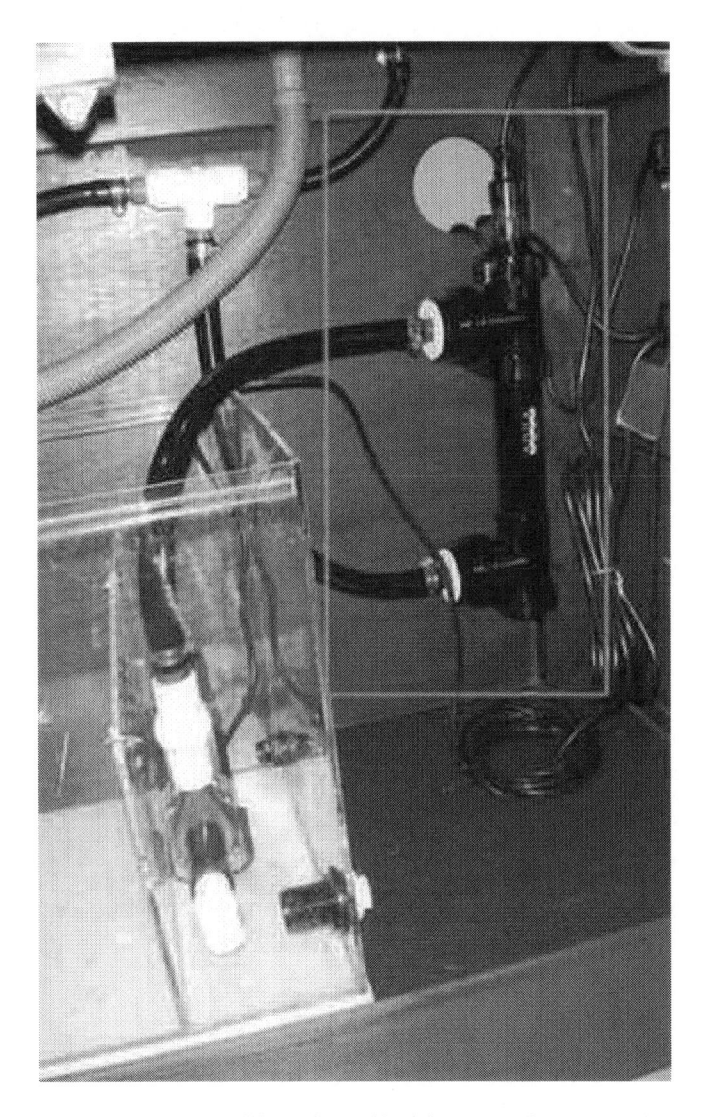

Inline UV sterilizer installed in aquarium stand

TIP: A UV light bulb needs to be changed on a regular basis. When installing an in-line UV, leave room to remove the light bulb or use clips which allows the UV sterilizer to tilt, to remove the light bulb.

Choosing and Stacking Live Rock

What is live rock and why use it?

Live rock is, as its name suggests, rock with living organisms (algae, bacteria, etc.) attached to it. Live rock comes from the ocean in different parts of the worlds such as Fiji, Marshall Islands, Tonga, Bali, Indo Pacific, and other tropical areas. It is usually named for the area in which it is found and harvested.

Fiji premium and Fiji shelf rock

Fiji branch and Fiji totoka

Fiji tukani and Real Reef Rock (manmade)

Many ecology-conscious entrepreneurs have begun to culture live rock by placing porous rock pieces on the ocean floor for a specified amount of time to allow algae, bacteria, animals and other organisms to grow in and on it. Whether natural or cultured, live rock brings natural biological properties from the ocean directly to your aquarium!

Some of the benefits of using live rock to aquascape your aquarium include the perhaps not so obvious biological benefits of increased surface area, and the introduction of helpful microorganisms, natural food sources, and living creatures that are found in the rock.

Is this live rock cured or uncured?

Live rock is removed from the ocean, placed in boxes and shipped through suppliers to aquarium stores. During shipping, much of the animal and plant life on the rock are damaged. When live rock is placed into an aquarium, the damaged and dying organisms create high levels of waste in the form of ammonia and nitrite, both of which are harmful to any live animals and plants that have survived the process.

Many pet and aquarium stores will take live rock from the ocean, "uncured" rock, through a process called "curing." If you choose to cure your own live rock see Appendix at the back of this guide.

Once the rock has gone through this process, it is called cured live rock. If possible, try to purchase cured rock and let the aquarium store suffer with the unavoidable rotten egg smell of the rock as it cures. Whether the rock you place in your aquarium is cured or uncured, it is important not to add any other animals until the ammonia and nitrite levels are zero. Uncured live rock takes 4 to 6 weeks before ammonia and nitrite levels return to zero. Cured rock may take a week or two before the levels drop.

TIP: Test ammonia and nitrite levels after adding live rock and before introducing fish. These levels must be zero before it is safe to add fish to your aquarium.

How much live rock do I need for my aquarium?

You can purchase live rock by the pound. The more porous the rock the lighter it is and the more surface area it has. It is a good rule of thumb to use one and a half to two pounds of rock per gallon of aquarium water. Personal preference and the density of the rock will determine how many pounds are needed.

Selecting live rock for your Aquarium

Choosing pieces to fit your tank

There are many ideas, preferences and opinions on how to aquascape with live rock. Some hobbyist prefer to place live rock flat across the bottom of the aquarium mimicking reef flat zones such as barrier reefs, atolls, fringes, or patch reefs. Others prefer to pile up rock in the center of their aquarium like islands mimicking outer reef edges like reef crests also known as shallow or upper reef slopes.

Stacking live rock

Another option is to stack rock high in the back of the aquarium simulating reef walls also known as fore reef slopes or deep reef slopes. This style is aesthetically pleasing, allowing the creation of large and small caverns for fish to swim through. It is versatile because it provides cliffs and areas on which to place live corals. It also allows you to place corals with regard to their needs, such as elevation, circulation, and lighting. This is the stacking method used in this book

In order to prepare to aquascape your aquarium choose a wide variety of pieces, as many different types of pieces as possible. Separate the pieces into three groups, which will be used to stack and aquascape the aquarium.

The groups are:
- Leg pieces (shaped like chair legs or cylinders), these pieces should be longer than they are wide and are used as legs to lift the main portion of the live rock off the

substrate. These pieces should not be so wide as to take up a lot of surface area on the bottom of the aquarium.
- Flat pieces (shaped like platters or plates), are great for bridges, whether parallel or at an incline to provide slopes in the aquarium. These pieces lie across leg pieces connecting to other pieces creating the look of a reef cliff.
- Bulk pieces are wider, larger pieces, generally somewhat round and sometimes having arms extending from them or curved in crazy directions. These odd shapes are fundamental to use to make aquascaping creative. These can also be used as mid-level leg pieces creating 2nd level bridges. You can also use them for facial or frontal pieces providing bulk (or reality) to the edging pieces, slopes, or even as top bridge pieces. In this way, their roundness provides depth to the aquarium as well as reality to the height (as if it is actually the top of a ridge.)

The order in which you add live rock, substrate and water can vary.

Option1 - First, stack live rock against the glass bottom of your aquarium and pour the substrate around the live rock . Finally add premixed saltwater.

Option2 - First add premixed saltwater or mix the saltwater inside the aquarium. Then stack live rock and pour the substrate around the rock.

Either of these techniques can ultimately lead to a successful saltwater and live rock aquarium. For the purpose of simplicity, this guide will explain the first technique in detail.

It is not a good idea to add substrate first because placing live rock on top of the substrate can make structures unstable. Some fish like to burrow and make tunnels and this can cause the rock to tumble. Stacking the rock first and pouring substrate around it creates a more stable structure, less susceptible to being toppled by the antics of burrowing creatures.

Stacking live rock on directly on bottom of aquarium

Stack rock in a sturdy fashion, yet loosely enough to keep water flowing through it. This will help your water quality. Also leave half to three-quarter of your substrate open (without rock covering it) to allow healthy water changes to pull out nutrients, organics and waste products from your aquarium. If you stack rock flat across the bottom of the tank or in the island fashion, it can be more difficult to extract waste from the substrate.

Whichever style of rock formation you choose here are a few rules to follow:
- Try to keep as much of the substrate open as possible.
- Make sure the rocks are stable. Use aquarium epoxy to help stabilize the rock.
- Build caves to allow the fish to feel relaxed.
- Use the rocks to hide filter and heaters to create a natural look.

It is interesting to note that live rock, pulled from the ocean, existed in a huge body of living, moving water. The ocean is what is called an open system, one in which water is constantly moving, washing away dirt, debris, nutrients, harmful chemicals, etc, and bringing in cleaner water. An aquarium is a closed system, one that does not have new water entering and old water exiting constantly. That is why we filter water in aquariums, to simulate the natural processes. In addition, we do water changes to remove wastes and debris.

Using Purified Water

Pure water is vital to the role in keeping our fish healthy. Reverse Osmosis (RO) and Reverse Osmosis with Deionization (RO/DI) is the preferred water for a reef. RO and RO/DI are processes used to clean city, municipal and well water using filter cartridges. Some reef hobbyist use city or municipal supplies however there are definite advantages to using RO and RO/DI.

Municipal and Well Water

Municipal water can contain chlorine or chloramines that must be neutralized before this water can be added to an aquarium. Besides chlorine compounds added by water treatment plants, there are many other impurities that can cause havoc to our living reef. Some of these impurities found in both municipal and well water include nitrates, phosphates, silicates, organic compounds, heavy metals and even toxins such as pesticides and fertilizers.

Nitrates, phosphates, and silicates are food for unwanted algae. Trying to keep algae under control in your reef when your water source is full of fertilizer (which causes algae to grow even faster than normal) can be very frustrating. Then there are the challenges caused by heavy metals. Trace amounts of some heavy metals are important for saltwater organisms to thrive, but as some levels increase, like copper for example, they can be fatal to corals, invertebrates and even fish. These are only a few of the risks that you take when using water straight from the tap. If you want to take control of the impurities in the water for your fish, use RO and RO/DI water.

Reverse Osmosis and Reverse Osmosis with Deionization

Reverse Osmosis (RO) and Reverse Osmosis with Deionization (RO/DI) are the purified waters of choice for most reef hobbyists. This water takes city or well water through a filtration process that removes 88% to 98% of the impurities. The process works by taking water through two pre-filter cartridges. One is a sediment cartridge to remove large debris; the other is a carbon cartridge to remove chlorine organic compounds and pesticides. Special cartridges are needed to remove chloramines. Water then passes through a semi-permeable membrane that is so dense that it allows only water molecules to pass through, leaving minerals, trace elements and other elements and compounds to be flushed away with wastewater. For each gallon of pure water that an RO unit produces, it also creates two to four gallons of wastewater.

Reverse osmosis system installed in cabinet

Reverse osmosis with deionization water filter installed under a home

Depending on the type of RO unit and the membrane used, as much as 92% dissolved solids water can be removed. Then, to get even cleaner water, some hobbyists add a deionization resin cartridge. After the water processes through the RO unit, it passes through the deionization resin and the resultant water is up to 98% pure.

Installing an RO unit in a home or office takes less than an hour. Some are even portable and can be attached directly to a faucet. If you choose not to purchase one, you can still purchase RO water at many aquarium stores. Just bring or buy containers to carry the water. If you ever question the purity of RO water, you can test it with a TDS meter, which indicates the level of total dissolved solids present. The lower the reading on the TDS meter the purer the water.

Remember, while a good salt mix is helpful, pure water makes all the difference!

Chapter 3

How to Assemble a Living Reef

This is the fun part: the actual reef assembly! And we are one step closer to adding our aquatic friends.

First, look at the equipment necessary to build our reef. Next, check out some optional products and finally, find a list of necessary test kits.

Equipment:
- Aquarium, drilled with overflow (at least 75 gallons)
- Aquarium stand
- Top with light or canopy
- Berlin sump or Berlin sump with refugium
- Return water pump
- Powerhead(s)
- Protein skimmer
- UV sterilizer
- Submersible heater
- Thermometer
- Substrate
- Marine salt
- Live rock (1 1/2 - 2 lbs. / gallon of aquarium water)
- Background (optional)
- Reverse osmosis water
- Bacteria starter
- 6-outlet power strip(s)
- Light timer(s)

Optional Products
- RO/DI filter System
- Wave maker

Test Kits and Equipment
- Hydrometer
- pH test kit
- Ammonia test kit
- Nitrite test kit
- Nitrate test kit
- Nitrate test kit
- Calcium test kit
- Carbonate hardness (Kh) test kit
- Phosphate test kit (optional)
- Syringe or dropper (optional)

Setting Up Your Mini Reef Aquarium

Step 1: Choose a Location for Your Aquarium

Choose a location that is **out of direct sunlight**. Aquariums that receive direct sunlight usually grow an abundance of algae and while this is not harmful to fish, invertebrates or corals, increased algae growth means more cleaning for you.

To keep your aquarium at a stable temperature, place the aquarium away from heating or cooling ducts as well as doorways leading to the outside. Keeping it out of direct sunlight also helps keep the temperature stable.

Aquarium with black end overflow on left allows viewing from front, back and right end

Make certain you have an electrical outlet near the aquarium.

NOTE: Reef aquariums can use a lot of current. Many high tech and large mini reef aquariums need their own dedicated circuit.

Choose a room where you spend a lot of time and where you can sit down and enjoy your aquarium.

Step 2: Leveling Your Aquarium

If you are using an existing piece of furniture on which to place your new aquarium be sure it is level, sturdy and will handle the weight of the aquarium when full. Water weighs approximately 8.3 pounds per gallon. A 90 gallon aquarium full of water will weigh at least 750 pounds! Add that 750 pounds to the weight of the substrate, live rock and the glass and this is a very heavy aquarium.

Make sure your aquarium is level front to back, side-to-side and corner-to-corner

Whether you have purchased an aquarium stand or are using existing furniture, be sure the base is level before you begin filling your aquarium. Once the aquarium is filled with water, it will be obvious if the tank is not level. This is not a good step on which to skimp.

Use a level. Level the aquarium front to back, side to side and corner to corner. Use shims (wooden or plastic wedges) under the stand at floor level until the tank is level.

NOTE: Level the stand with shims between the floor and the stand, never between the stand and the aquarium.

When installing the aquarium on carpet most of the time wood or metal strips are used to secure the carpet and keep it flat. These strips are installed close to a wall. If the aquarium is placed on a strip, it will raise up the back of the aquarium. If possible, space the aquarium from the wall in front of the strip.

Once shims are placed under the stand and the tank reads level, you are ready to move on.

Step 3: Preparing the Aquarium

Using a soft cloth or damp paper towel, wipe down the inside of the aquarium to remove dirt and dust.

CAUTION: NEVER use soap or household cleaning agents in or on your aquarium. Even the most thorough rinse may not remove all chemicals left on the glass when using toxic cleaning products.

Step 4: Adding a Background

The background is attached to the outside back of the aquarium to hide the filter and electrical cords. It adds depth to your tank and can create a pleasing setting. Clean and dry the back of the aquarium to prepare it for the background. Cut the background to the exact length of the aquarium. Use clear tape. Attach the right and left sides to your aquarium. Next, attach the top edge of the background with tape. Run a piece of tape the whole length of the top of the aquarium to keep water that may splash from the tank from forming spots between the background and the aquarium glass.

Step 5: Install Plumbing Kit in Overflow Box

Predrilled aquariums have at least two holes drilled in the bottom. One hole is plumbed to drain water from the aquarium and the other hole is plumbed to return water to the aquarium. These holes are enclosed in the aquarium by an overflow box. For additional information, see Chapter 2.

Our example uses an aquarium with the overflow attached to the back glass of an aquarium.

Back view of aquarium with overflow box and two holes in bottom of aquarium (not visible)

It is time to install the plumbing in the drain and return holes. Most aquarium manufacturers have overflow plumbing kits. Here is an example of the plumbing.

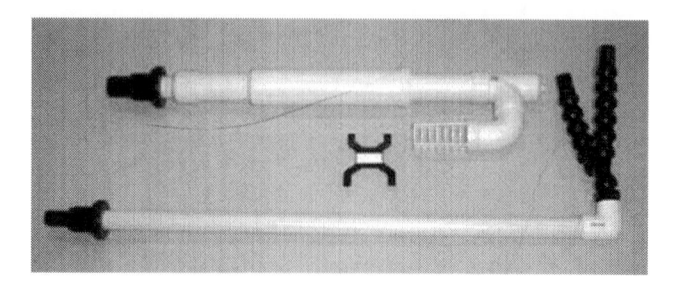

Drain and return assembly

Since each aquarium manufacturer has a different plumbing kit, just follow their directions to assemble and install in the aquarium.

Here is a finished view of drain and return installed.

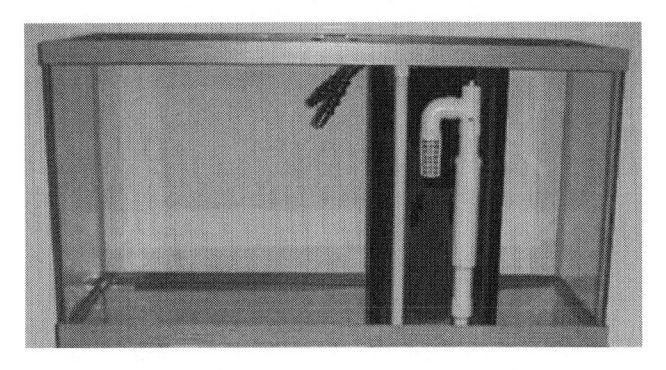

Return assembly (thinner white tube on left) and drain assembly (larger white tube on right) installed

Step 6: Installing Filtration

A saltwater aquarium with live rock should use a Berlin filter. A Berlin filter has a sump (holding chamber) with a mechanical filter and space for a protein skimmer and other equipment. A Berlin filter is placed below the aquarium usually in a cabinet stand.

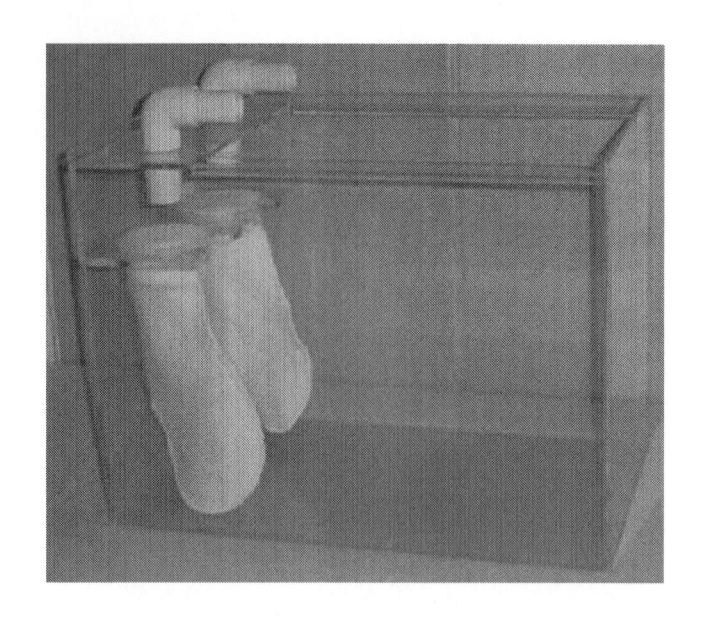

Basic - Berlin sump with 2 sock hangers and filter socks

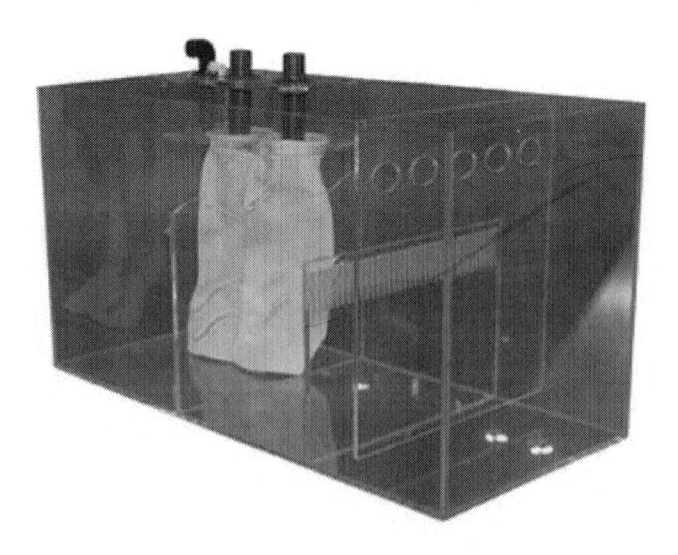

Deluxe - Berlin sump has two sock hangers, refugium, protein skimmer and return water pump compartments

Place filter below aquarium in cabinet.

Placing Berlin sump in cabinet

TIP: A piece of Styrofoam placed under a Berlin sump will allow the filter to level itself and remove any unevenness from the stand.

The aquarium has its overflow plumbing kits installed and the filter is in the cabinet below the aquarium. Let's look at how the aquarium and filter work together.

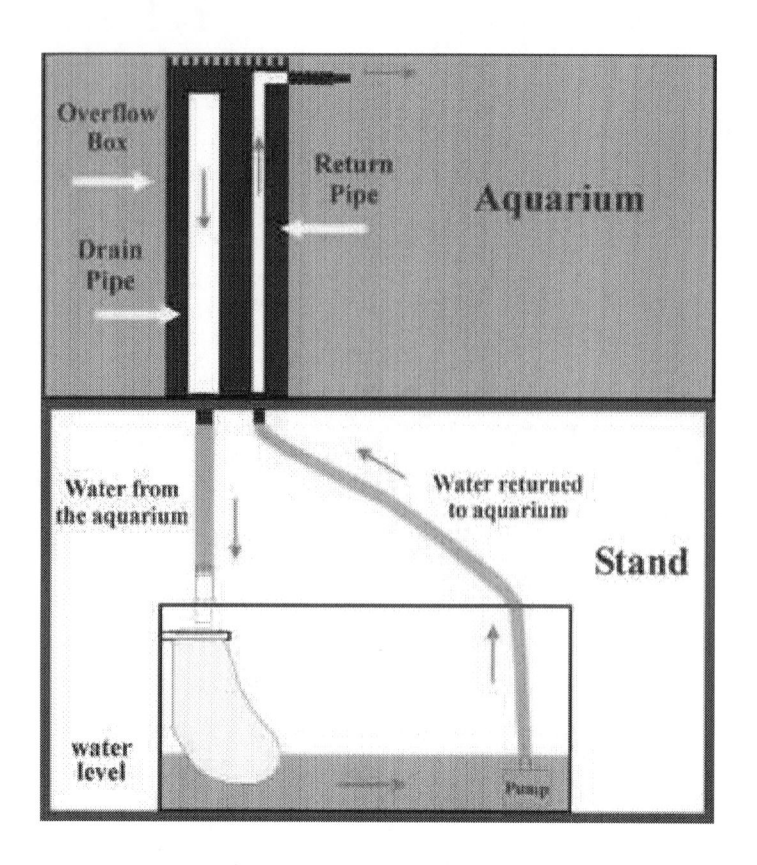

Diagram of installed Berlin sump and water flow

This diagram shows how water is routed from the overflow box of the aquarium through a drain line down to the Berlin filter. It is pre-filtered through a filter sock and returned to the aquarium via a water pump.

Here is the general way to install a Berlin sump. Berlin sumps typically have one or two connections on the top of the sump designed to be attached to the drain line(s) of your drilled aquarium.

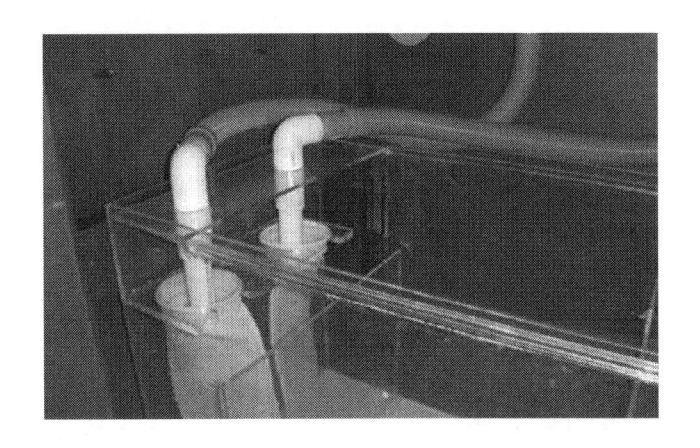

Two vacuum hoses attached to Berlin filter

If you are using pre-manufactured drain lines such as vacuum hose, position the sump inside your cabinet so that the drain lines form as straight path as possible from the bottom of your overflow chamber to the drain line connections on the top of your sump.

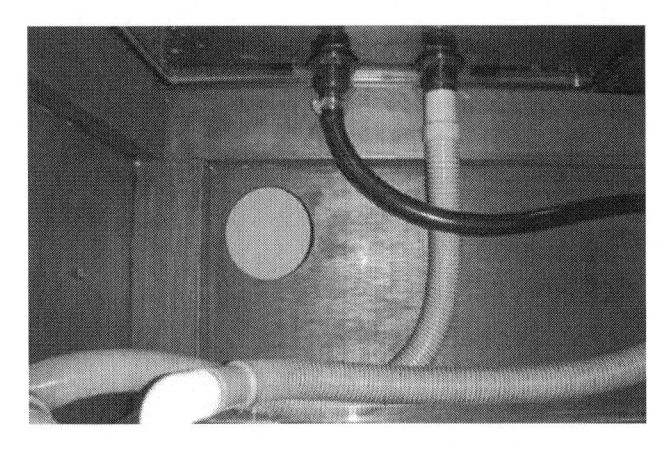

Gray vacuum line attached to drain line from aquarium

These drain lines should not drop below the top of the Berlin sump before connecting to the sump, as debris and air can collect in these areas and interfere with proper drainage from the aquarium. If your drain line is too long to make a straight path from the overflow bulkhead to your sump, loop the drain line in such a manner as to ensure water is always traveling down toward your sump.

Most pre-manufactured drain lines are made to fit one-inch PVC attachments on the top of sumps, and can be pressure fit to the drainage attachment on the sump. Because these lines are not under pressure, it is not necessary to use hose clamps. But, it never hurts to secure a hose clamp to all tubing.

Once the drain line is securely attached to the Berlin filter and the drain bulkhead of your display tank, the drainage of your aquarium to the Berlin filter is complete.

Step 7: Installing the Return Pump

Overflow boxes skim water off the surface of an aquarium and channel the water down to a Berlin filter. A pump then returns the water to your aquarium. The pump can be internal (placed inside the sump) or external (outside the sump).

Installing your return pump and plumbing is largely dependent upon your particular sump and configuration.

Internal Water Pump

Internal pumps have a return outlet that is either threaded or slip. This means you can thread a plastic fitting onto the threaded outlet or attach flexible tubing to the slip outlet. If your pump is a little too powerful for your aquarium a ball valve may be used to adjust the water flow. Threaded fittings on a pump make it convenient to thread a ball valve directly to the pump. Use Teflon tape on all the threads to make a waterproof seal. Once the ball valve is attached choose the size fitting you will need to run your return tubing back to your aquarium. If your aquarium has a bulkhead to return the water to your aquarium then make sure your flexible tubing is the correct size.

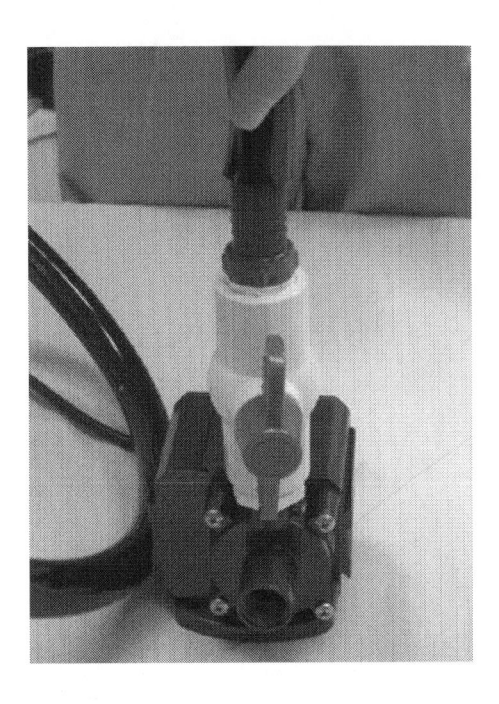

Internal pump with ball valve, poly fitting and flexible tubing

Make sure your flexible tubing attaches to your return fittings. Make your return line as straight as possible. The more bends increases the head pressure therefore reducing the water flow from the pump.

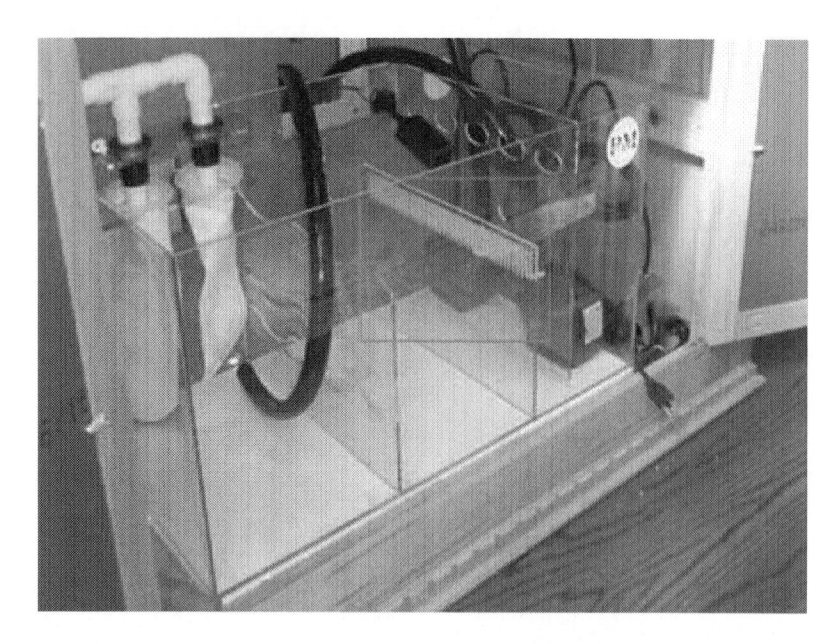

Internal pump in back of last chamber on right, highlighted by green outline. Front pump in right chamber goes to remote chiller

One side of the flexible tubing is attached to the pump the other side attaches to the return line sticking out the bottom of the aquarium.

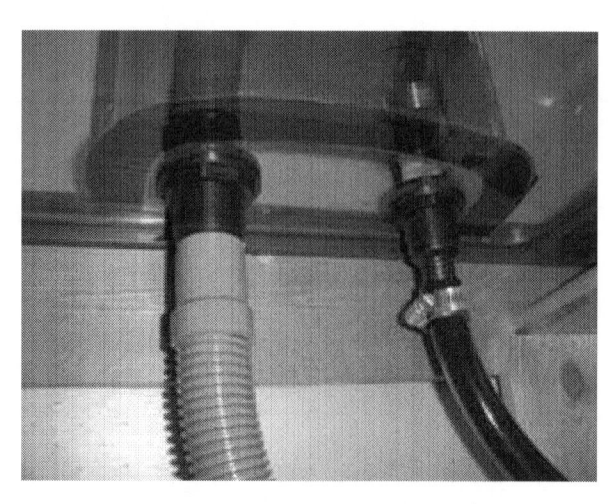

Grey tubing attached to bulkhead drain from aquarium. Water pump attached to right water return

External Water Pump

An external pump should be placed on a flat, dry surface next to the sump. If the pump does not have a rubber pad or feet then place a small layer of rubber or foam under the pump to minimize vibration. Some sumps come pre-drilled to accommodate external pump. Others, you must use a hole saw and drill your own hole. Just use a bulkhead to slide through the hole in the filter to attach an external pump.

If using a bulkhead then you can use either pvc fittings with flexible tubing or you may choose to plumb with standard PVC pipe and fittings.

External pump plumbed into a Berlin filter

TIP: To make it easy to remove or change an external water pump, use a true union ball valve between the intake side or the pump and the filter and another true union ball valve between the output side of the pump and the return tubing (not shown.)

Step 8 - Install a Power Strip

Mount power strip(s) inside the cabinet or other protected place. Laying a power strip on the floor behind an aquarium stand is risky as there is then the chance that water could accidentally spill on it. Saltwater and electricity make a bad combination.

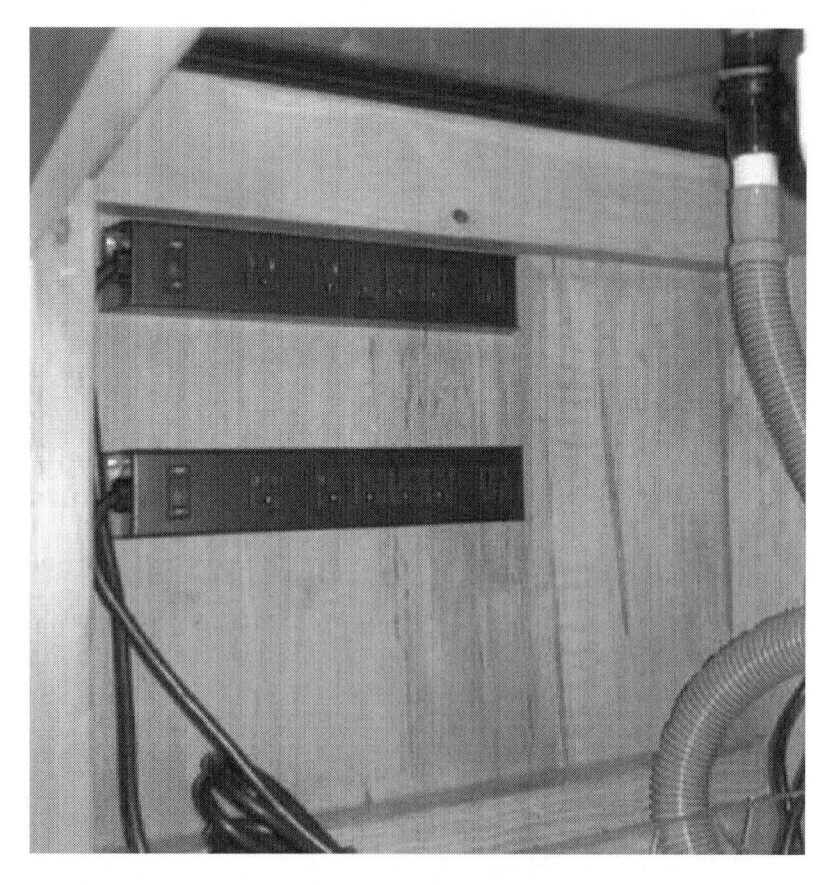

Power strips with surge protectors mounted in cabinet

If you have your aquarium sitting on top of a desk or shelf, make sure no water can ever splash on the power outlet or power strip. Do not plug power outlet strip into wall receptacle at this time.

Step 9 - Install Protein Skimmer

Protein skimmers physically remove dissolved organic compounds and other substances from aquarium water. Assemble the protein skimmer following manufacturer's directions. Place the protein skimmer in the Berlin sump as shown. **Do not plug it in at this time.**

Internal protein skimmer in compartment with prefilter socks

Step 10 - Adding Live rock

There are many ways to stack live rock to mimic ocean reefs (this is discussed Choosing and Stacking Live Rock.) The stacking method we will use is the fore-reef slopes where the rock is stacked high in the back of the aquarium simulating reef walls. This style is aesthetically pleasing and allows the creation of large and/or small caverns for fish to swim through as well as cliffs and shelves at varying depths to place live corals. Corals can be placed on these cliffs and shelves with regard to their needs, such as elevation, circulation, and lighting.

Place live rock directly on glass

It is not a good idea to add substrate first because placing Live Rock on top of the substrate can make structures unstable. Some fish like to burrow and make tunnels and this can cause the rock to tumble. Stacking the rock first and pouring substrate around it creates a more stable structure, less susceptible to being toppled by the antics of burrowing creatures.

Stack rock in a sturdy fashion, yet loosely enough to keep water flowing through it. This will help your water quality. Also leave ½ to ¾ of your substrate open (without rock covering it) to allow healthy water changes to pull out nutrients, organics and waste products from your aquarium.

Note crevices and small caves

Flat rock inserted between two other rocks creating a perfect shelf for a coral

An example of stacked rock - it is not too impressive looking at this point!

When stacking live rock, sometimes it will look like a pile of rocks when you finish. As long as you have some caves, crevices and shelves, your rockwork will work fine. If you are not happy with the way your rockwork looks, simply make changes. Since livestock will not be added until The Cycle (see Water Quality Explained) is complete, you have time to move a couple of rocks around. Once corals are added, the rockwork will look a lot different.

Completed Rock Stack in a 210 gallon aquarium

Here is an example of an island live rock stacking. In this picture, the aquarium will be viewed from the front and back, rocks are stacked in the center of the aquarium without touching the walls

Whichever style of rock formation you choose here are a few rules to follow:
- Try to keep as much of the substrate open as possible.
- Make sure the rocks are stable. Use aquarium epoxy to help stabilize the rock.
- Build caves to allow fish to feel relaxed.
- Use the rocks to hide filter parts (if they are in the aquarium) and to create a natural look.

When stacking live rock you may find that you need a certain shape rock or a certain size rock. Live rock is usually easy to break and shape. A hammer and a chisel will easily break the rock to a smaller size and it is easy to shape a rock to be more stable (wear safety glasses.) If your rock stack is still not stable, use reef epoxy.

Reef epoxy is available in grey, pink or purple and will bond rocks to each other. Epoxy is also a great way to secure live corals to live rock.

Applying purple-colored epoxy to live rock for support

Step 11 - Adding Substrate

The substrate you choose should be made of aragonite, a beneficial substrate that slowly dissolves and releases buffers to help keep the pH at an acceptable level for the livestock. Some substrates are clean and require no pre-rinsing.

A popular choice is called live sand. This is coral reef sand either collected live from the ocean or commercially manufactured. Manufactured live sands are readily available and are sands populated with live nitrifying bacteria. The live bacteria should speed up the time an aquarium takes to cycle (ready for livestock.) Live sand should not be rinsed.

Another choice of substrate is packaged dry. This substrate may be dusty or dirty simply rinse it in a large bucket, 10 to 15 pounds at a time. Run clean tap water through it, stir and drain it to wash away dust and debris. You may also use a kitchen colander.

Sand are available in many sizes. We will choose a one to two mm size sand since this works for most fish and invertebrates and is easy to vacuum during maintenance.

Some aquarists prefer a deep substrate bed. For our purposes, we will add enough substrate to create a one" to two" thick layer.

Spreading out the substrate

Pour aragonite into an open spot on the floor of the aquarium. Then spread it evenly on the bottom of the aquarium to a depth of one to two inch thick.

Step 12 - The Heater
Set the dial on your submersible heater, to a specific temperature and a thermostat inside the heater will keep the temperature constant. Because there are many heater manufacturers, it is best to follow their specific instructions to set and attach your heater. Place the heater in

the sump with the suction cups against the bottom. The suction cups will elevate the heater from the surface of the sump so that water can circulate completely around it. This will permit the heater to work efficiently. **DO NOT plug the heater in to an outlet before adding water!**

Submersible heater placed in sump. Suction cups are facing up. Heater needs to be rotated and suction cups attached to bottom of sump

Set the temperature between 80° and 82°F until a biological foundation is established. Once your aquarium is cycled (see Water Quality Explained) set the temperature to between 76° and 78°F.

Step 13 - Power head

Power head installation: Power heads help circulate water and increase the current in the aquarium; they keep water flowing through the Live rock, reminiscent of the flow of water in the ocean.

Power heads can be installed on the side or back panes of glass, on either or both sides of the aquarium.

90 gallon reef with three powerheads in green squares

NOTE: Power heads need to be cleaned regularly. They can be hid by live rock just make sure they can be easily removed for cleaning.

Step 14 - Adding Water

Since Reverse Osmosis (RO) and Reverse Osmosis with Deionization (RO/DI) water are the best choices, this is what we will use. RO water and RO water mixed with marine salt is often sold in 5-gallon jugs at local fish and pet stores. You can also purchase your own RO filter system (see Using Purified Water for more information.)

If you purchase premixed RO water from the store, the water should be ready to pour into your aquarium. Allow water to become room temperature.

Adding premixed saltwater

> **TIP: When using live rock and live sand substrate you MUST mix the salt and water before adding it to the aquarium. (If you add freshwater directly to your live sand, you can kill the beneficial bacteria in the sand.)**

Mixing Your Own Saltwater

If you have your own RO filter system, you must premix your saltwater before adding it to the aquarium. Begin by filling a 5-gallon bucket or larger non-toxic container (preferably with wheels) with RO water. Next, add salt to the water. Follow the instructions on the salt mix, keeping in mind that a general rule is to add approximately one cup of salt to every two gallons of aquarium water.

After mixing salt with the water in the bucket, use a hydrometer to test specific gravity. There are two different types of hydrometers that aquarists use. One is a plastic box with a floating swing-arm and the other looks similar to a floating glass thermometer. Either style will work.

The specific gravity should read between 1.023 and 1.025. If the specific gravity is too low, add more salt. If you add too much salt and the hydrometer reads over the target, remove some of the water and add fresh RO water.

The RO filter system should have removed chlorine and/or chloramines, therefore a water conditioner is not necessary. Test pH and make sure it is between 8.2 and 8.4. If the pH is below 8.2, add a buffering agent to adjust it. (More information about pH can be found in Water Quality Explained)

Pour water slowly onto one of the live rocks close to the bottom of the aquarium. (Since you just spread out the substrate, you do not want to blow it all around.) You can also place a dinner plate in the aquarium temporarily on which to pour the water. Fill the aquarium until the water level is just above the bottom of the aquarium's frame and water begins to flow over the overflow.

At this point you can either continue to add water to the aquarium to fill the Berlin sump in the cabinet or you can pour water directly into the sump until filled to the designated max fill line.

For **larger aquariums**, carrying water back and forth may take too much time and energy. You may want to purchase a new thirty-five to forty-five gallon trashcan or other non-toxic, plastic container (with wheels.) Whichever size container you choose it should **only** be used for your aquarium. Once the salt is mixed in the container, roll it over to the aquarium. The premixed saltwater can either be bucketed into the aquarium or a water pump with flexible tubing attached can be used to pump the water into the aquarium.

Step 15 - Setting Up a Refugium

In our example, we are using a refugium built into a Berlin sump. A built-in refugium is usually a compartment in a Berlin sump which houses mud or sand and algae. The walls of the compartment are made to allow water to pass through and return to the display aquarium. These walls also slow water flow to assist with macro algae feeding.

The size of the refugium needed depends on the bio-load of the display aquarium. A larger refugium is necessary for a heavily stocked aquarium; smaller refugium may be used for a lightly stocked aquarium.

Refugiums are easy to setup just add mud and/or an oolithic (sugar size) aragonite sand to a depth of up to six inches and macro algae.

Refugium compartment with oolithic sand

Place a light over the refugium to help grow macro algae. The bulb should be 5,000 to 6,500 Kelvin for optimum plant growth.

Choose a light fixture that produces at least 4 watts per gallon of water in the refugium (for those less than 16 inches deep.)

Two T5 strip lights mounted above refugium

NOTE: Set the refugium light to turn on when the aquarium light goes off (for more information see Refugium.)

Macro algae can be added to refugium 24 hours after aquarium is setup or you can wait until reef has "cycled". Chaetomorpha, Ulva (Sea Lettuce), halimeda (red seaweed) and Gracilaria (red seaweed) are macro algae that do well in refugiums.

Step 16 - Starting the Equipment

It is time to plug in the water pump, which returns water to the aquarium into an electrical outlet. The water should start leaving the sump and flow into the aquarium. Soon water will flow back down into the sump over the overflow box. Add water to the sump if need to until it reaches the fill line on the side of the Berlin sump.

Sump is filled with premixed saltwater to the correct height

Plug in to an electrical outlet the water pump on the protein skimmer and follow manufacturer's directions to properly adjust your protein skimmer.

Install a Thermometer
Attach a hanging thermometer to the aquarium or inside the Berlin sump. Do not put a thermometer in the return pump compartment if you do not have a prefilter on the pump.

Keep a thermometer in the aquarium or sump as it allows you to ensure the heater works properly and, during the warm months, it helps you keep tabs that the aquarium is not getting too hot.

NOTE: A thermometer is also necessary for water changes. When you change aquarium water, you want to make sure the new water is within two degrees of the temperature of the water in your aquarium.

Plug in the Heater

Once the water is in the sump, wait ten to fifteen minutes before plugging in the heater to allow the temperature of the heater's glass tube to acclimate to the temperature of the water. This will prevent the glass tube from cracking due to a rapid change in temperature.

SAFETY TIP: Make sure any electrical wires leading from your filter, heater, and lights to an electrical outlet have drip loops. If a drop of water travels down your cord it will drip at the bottom of the loop before it enters your electrical socket. Electrical cords, when plugged into the electrical outlet, must loop below the outlet.

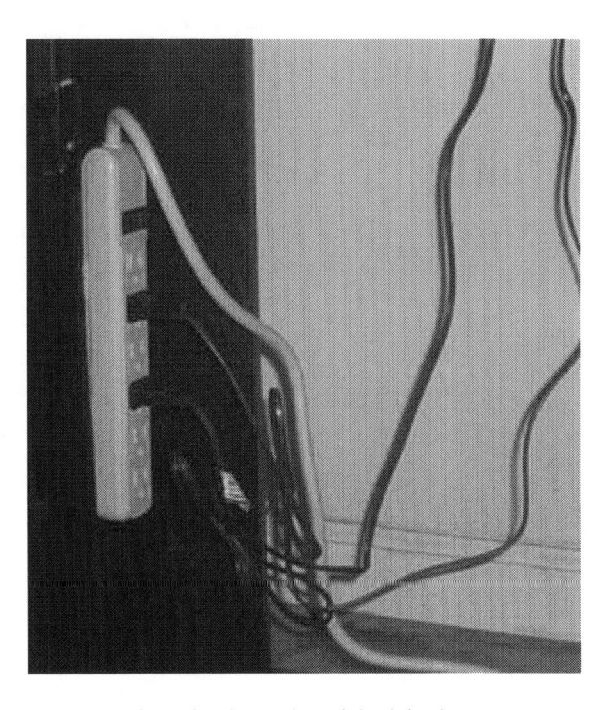

Electrical cords with drip loop

Step 17 - Placing the Canopy and Light

There are many choices when it comes to reef lighting. The reef in our setup has a wooden canopy to match the stand. The inside of the canopy has been sealed to make it water proof. Lights are mounted directly in the canopy. In this case we have 2 x 250 watt metal halides and 4 x 54 watt t5 actinic lights. Fixtures all have reflectors to increase and direct the light.

Light fixtures and lamps installed in canopy. Blue color from actinic T5 fluorescent lamps

NOTE: The aquarium above is four feet long and canopy opens completely in front for easy access. This is beneficial when cleaning or working on your reef.

If you are using un-cured live rock, the lights should remain off until rock has cycled. If you are using cured live rock, you can have your lights on for a couple of hours a day. Lots of light can cause unwanted algae growing in your aquarium. Reducing the light to a few hours a day will help control algae growth. When water has cycled and livestock has been added, than the lights can run for 6 to 10 hours a day. How long the lights are on is determined by the type of light you use.

In our example, we will follow the pattern of sunrise to sunset. We will set the actinic lights (blue lamps) to turn on in the morning first. Using a timer, they will be set to turn on at 8:00 am. Two hours later at 10:00 am, the halide lights will turn on. The halide lights will stay on for six to eight hours and go off. About two hours later the actinic lights are turned off. The halides produce intense full spectrum lights much like the sun.

Step 18 - The Final Step

The reef is completely setup, stand back & enjoy your creation!

Reef completely assembled

Island stacked reef completely assembled. Water will be crystal clear within 24 hours

At this point, your aquarium is completely setup. Now is the perfect time to learn a about water quality and testing equipment.

Once the live rock has cycled (discussed in next Water Quality Explained), you are ready to do a partial water change and add some livestock!

Chapter 4

Water Quality Explained

Good water quality is essential to keeping fish, corals and invertebrates healthy and alive for years.

Why test water?

Our goal is to create an environment in which our mini reef will thrive. The only way to determine if the quality of the aquarium water is ideal is to test it.

What needs to be tested?

The basic tests to perform regularly on aquarium water are pH, ammonia, nitrite, nitrate, calcium and KH and specific gravity.

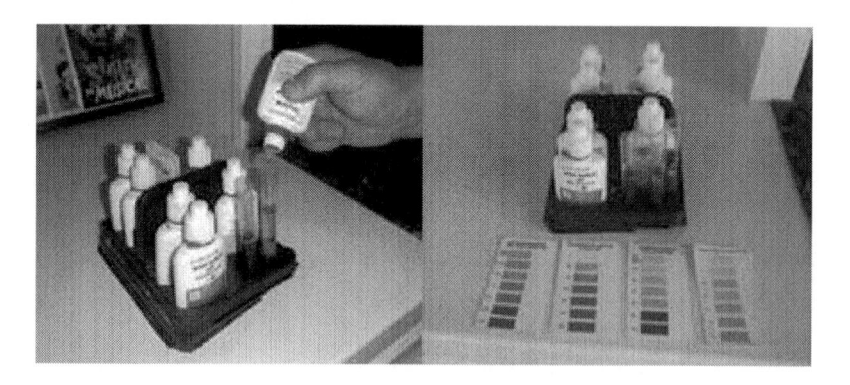

The majority of aquarium test kits are easy to use

Let us look at why these tests are necessary.

pH and KH

A simple understanding of pH is helpful to keep your fish healthy. The term pH refers to how acidic or basic a substance is. The pH scale ranges from 0 to 14 with 7 is neutral. A pH reading lower than 7 indicates an acid, a reading higher than 7 indicates a base.

pH Scale

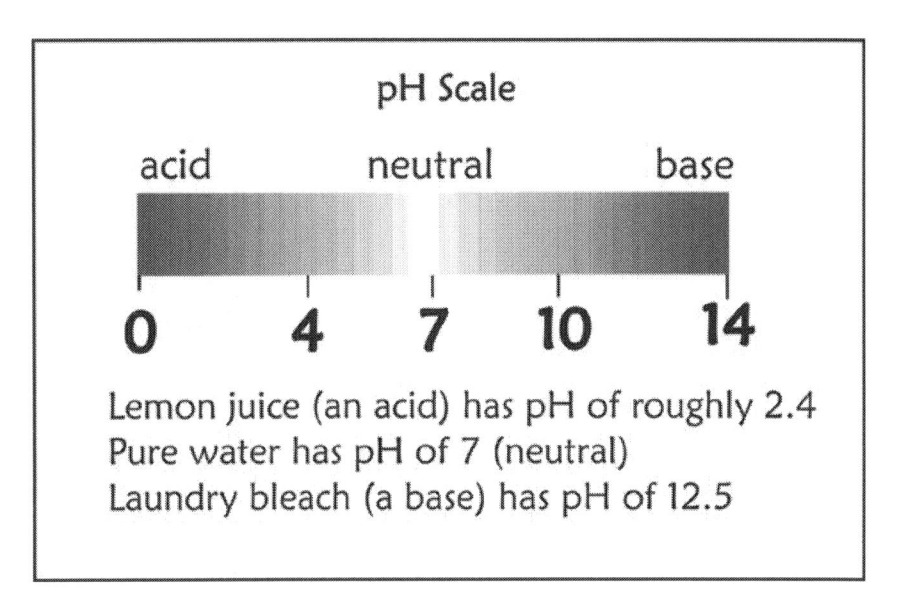

acid — neutral — base

0   4   7   10   14

Lemon juice (an acid) has pH of roughly 2.4
Pure water has pH of 7 (neutral)
Laundry bleach (a base) has pH of 12.5

Saltwater fish, invertebrates and coral need a higher pH than most freshwater fish

For a living reef, the optimal pH level is 8.2 - 8.4. It is prudent to test aquarium water and adjust pH, if necessary, before adding livestock. Most aquatic animals prefer gradual changes in pH. To maintain a high and stable pH in water we must learn a little about Alkalinity. Alkalinity is the buffering capacity of a body of water. It measures the ability of aquarium water to neutralize acids and bases thereby maintaining a fairly stable pH.

Saltwater contains compounds, such as bicarbonates and carbonates, which combine with H+ ions from the water thereby raising the pH of the water. Without this buffering capacity, any acid added to the water would immediately decrease the pH.

To maintain an ideal pH level in a reef aquarium requires a higher alkalinity. High alkalinity means that the aquarium water has the ability to neutralize acids from fish, corals and invertebrate waste, decaying fish food, etc.

We use a Carbonate Hardness (KH) test kit to measure Alkalinity. If the KH measures between 8 and 13 dKH, the pH in the reef should remain stable. If the KH is lower than 8, there are many products available to increase it; choose one and follow directions carefully. Should a change in pH be necessary, add a reef buffering agent. There are many buffering agents on the market;

Specific Gravity

There are two different types of hydrometers used to test specific gravity, which measure the salt levels in a reef aquarium. One is a plastic box with a floating swing-arm and the other looks similar to a floating glass thermometer. Either style will work. Follow the manufacturers' directions and test your specific gravity.

Specific gravity should read between 1.023 and 1.025. If it is too low, add more salt. If you add too much salt and the hydrometer reads over the target, remove some of the water and add fresh water.

The Nitrogen Cycle

Once live rock is assembled and sand added to your aquarium, your tank will begin a process called The Nitrogen Cycle (we will just call it The Cycle for short.) The Cycle does not begin until there are waste products from live rock present in the water. This waste product is produced from once live, now deceased and decaying organisms on live rock. Their deaths are caused by shipping, handling and even just moving the rock from one aquarium to another.

As live rock is prepared for transport, shippers wrap it in newspaper to preserve the moisture. Even so, much of the sea life on the rock quickly begins to dry out. When packed in shipping boxes, the rocks rub against each other killing even more sea life in those spots.

Deceased life, whether animal, bacteria or plant, decays, producing waste that is toxic to fish. This waste product begins in the form of ammonia and, if left unchecked, the fish, corals and invertebrates would simply die.

Thankfully, nature has a relatively simple and natural system that will keep our animals alive. While harmful to livestock, ammonia provides food to bacteria, called nitrosomonas, which are very beneficial in an aquarium. These bacteria break down ammonia into something called nitrite.

Nitrite is also harmful to livestock, but as luck would have it, yet another naturally occurring bacteria, nitrospira, uses harmful nitrite and gives off a byproduct called nitrate.

Nitrate is less toxic than either ammonia or nitrite.

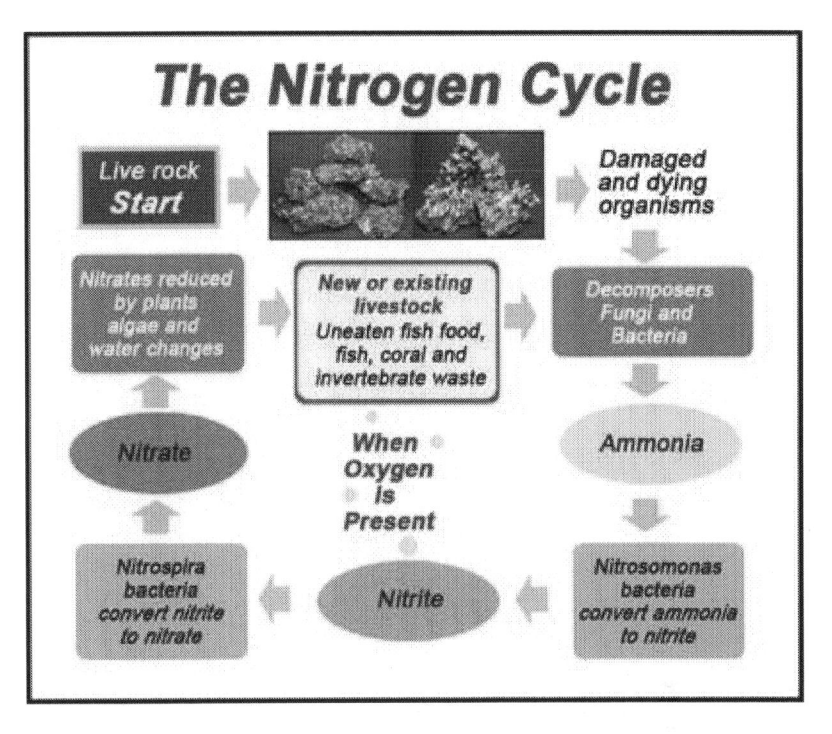

The Nitrogen Cycle

- Live rock **Start** → [rock image] → Damaged and dying organisms
- Damaged and dying organisms → Decomposers Fungi and Bacteria
- Decomposers Fungi and Bacteria → Ammonia
- Ammonia → Nitrosomonas bacteria convert ammonia to nitrite
- Nitrosomonas bacteria → Nitrite
- Nitrite → Nitrospira bacteria convert nitrite to nitrate
- Nitrospira bacteria → Nitrate
- Nitrate → Nitrates reduced by plants, algae and water changes
- Nitrates reduced by plants, algae and water changes → New or existing livestock: Uneaten fish food, fish, coral and invertebrate waste
- When Oxygen Is Present

Flowchart of The Nitrogen Cycle

It takes two to six weeks for beneficial bacteria to become established when the aquarium water is 80°F. This process may take longer at lower temperatures. Because high levels of ammonia and nitrite are stressful to livestock, no animals should be introduced once The Cycle begins. After The Cycle finishes (when both ammonia and nitrite levels are zero), a partial water change is recommended (see How to Care for a Reef) and now the livestock can then be added.

A protein skimmer is very beneficial at removing a lot of the organic waste before it is broken down into ammonia.

Several bacteria starters are on the market today that can shorten cycling time. These products contain live cultures of beneficial bacteria; add them directly to aquarium water at the same time you add live rock to jump-start the bacteria that occur naturally.

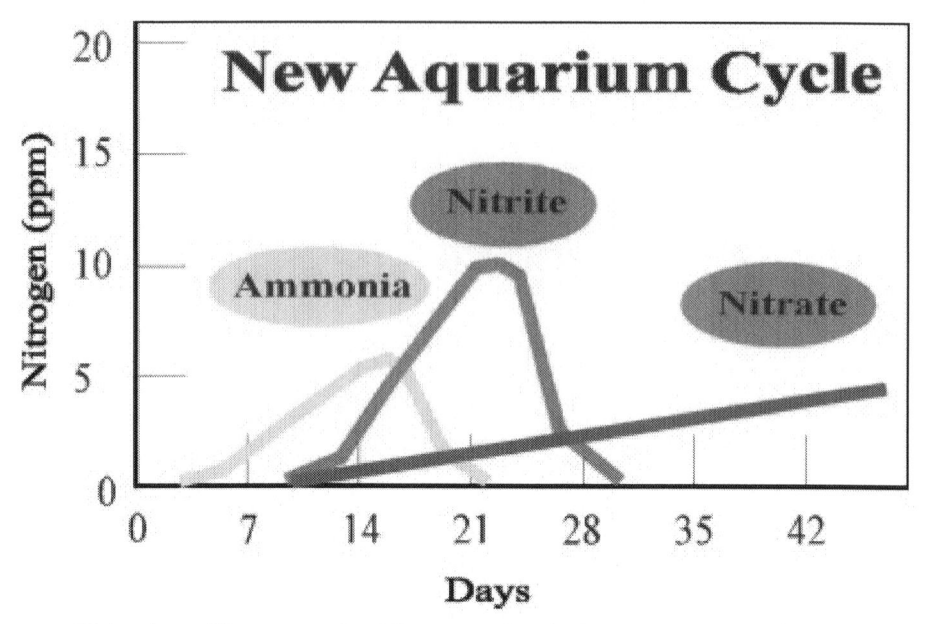

New Aquarium Cycle

Nitrogen (ppm) vs. Days — showing Ammonia, Nitrite, and Nitrate curves

This chart illustrates the Nitrogen Cycle Process. Actual levels of ammonia, nitrite and nitrate may vary. Many factors determine these levels: whether the live rock is cured or uncured, if a protein skimmer is used, the temperature of the water and how quickly beneficial bacteria become established.

You now see why test kits are helpful in determining where the levels are during The Cycle. Ammonia and nitrite test kits will determine harmful compound levels so that we know when the aquarium is ready for livestock. You can see that ammonia and nitrite are controlled biologically by beneficial bacteria and with a protein skimmer. It can also be reduced by water changes (see How to Care for a Reef.) Normally we do not change water when cycling with cured live rock.

Once beneficial bacteria are established, it is safe to add fish, corals or inverts a few at a time to allow "good" bacteria to keep up with the increase of waste. If too much livestock is added, there may be toxic spikes in ammonia or nitrite.

Nitrate

As we just discussed, the byproduct of the Nitrogen Cycle is nitrates. Nitrates build up slowly over time. Even a low level of nitrate can be harmful to corals and invertebrates. To keep this level in check, use a nitrate test kit. If the results read less than 10 ppm, then all is well. If Nitrate level needs to be reduced, accomplish this through water changes (with low or zero nitrate replacement water), reduce the amount of food you are feeding your fish, remove any dead fish, inverts or decaying plant matter, replace nitrate-removing media to just name a few.

NOTE: micro and macro algae (plants) use nitrates as a food source.

Let's assume at this point our aquarium pH and specific gravity are correct, our live rock has cycled and temperature is 78 degrees.

Are we ready for livestock?

We can safely add fish, some invertebrates and soft corals but we need to run a few more test before we add stony corals.

Calcium

Some of the most beautiful corals in the reef are Stony corals. Stony corals have skeletons made from Calcium and Carbonate. For stony corals to grow there must be plenty of both of these compounds available in our aquarium water. The experts have discovered that for corals to grow properly there needs to be between 400 and 450 ppm calcium in the water. To find how much calcium is in our reef aquarium we test the water with a calcium test kit.

Corals are not the only one using calcium, fish use it to make their skeleton and invertebrates, like snails, make their shells with calcium; even some soft corals use calcium to create spicules. Calcium levels can be depleted quickly in an established reef.

Test calcium in your reef, if low add a calcium additive. Calcium additives are available in liquid or powdered form. Follow manufacturer's directions for dosing.

Our corals need both Calcium and Carbonate to make their stony skeletons, so it is critical to test both Calcium and Carbonate and keep both of levels in the recommend ranges. If either level decreases, corals will not have building blocks to create their skeleton.

Magnesium

Calcium and Carbonate bind easily to each other. This is a good thing for corals, but these calcium carbonate compounds can also attach to each other and can then precipitate out of solution. This means they will not be available for the corals to use to create their skeleton. Nature is brilliant; it has come up with a solution: Magnesium. It is very simple; if you want high levels of Calcium and Carbonate in your reef, keep high levels of Magnesium. Magnesium levels should stay between 1200 and 1320 ppm. This test kit is optional because if you are able to keep Calcium and Carbonate levels up, then you know there is enough Magnesium available. Magnesium is also available at most stores with given dosages for your size aquarium.

Minor Trace Elements

There are many minor trace elements in seawater like Iodine, Iodide, Iron, etc., several of which have noticeable effect on coral growth and coloration. Before delving into complex water chemistry, make sure all major trace elements like Calcium, Magnesium, Strontium, Carbonate are at their optimum levels. A good grade of reef salt contains many of these minor trace elements. Partial water changes (see How to Care for a Reef) will replenish many minor trace elements used by reef livestock.

Recommended Reef Aquarium Water Parameters

Temperature	76 to 78 degrees Fahrenheit
Specific Gravity	1.023 to 1.025
pH	8.2 to 8.4
Ammonia	0 ppm
Nitrite	0 ppm
Nitrate	< 10 ppm
Alkalinity	8 and 13 dKH
Calcium	400 and 450 ppm
Magnesium	1200 and 1320 ppm
Phosphate	0 ppm
Iodine	0.5 to 0.8 ppm
Iron	0.1 to 0.3 ppm

Chart of recommended reef aquarium water parameters.

NOTE: As corals grow and bio loads increase, use your test kits to determine how much additive your aquarium water requires. Manufacturer's recommendations are just that recommendations. Testing your aquarium water ensures there are enough major elements available for healthy corals and invertebrates growth.

FREE BONUS: To get your FREE Water Testing Tracking Form, go to http://9nl.be/FreeReefBonuses

Once our water is ideal we can get to the fun part - adding livestock. Let us begin with Reef safe fish.

Chapter 5

How to Choose Fish for a Reef

After the Nitrogen Cycle has finished, you have completed a partial water change (see How to Care for a Reef), specific gravity is between 1.023 and 1.025, and pH is between 8.2 and 8.4, it is now time to add some livestock. A partial water change may not be necessary if your cycle was very mild and lasted for less than a couple of weeks. If the water is not clear, see How to Care for a Reef.

Throughout the following pages you will find general descriptions of some of the more popular reef-safe fish. You will learn about the diets of many species, whether they are carnivores, herbivores or omnivores. Carnivorous fish eat meat; herbivores eat algae, seaweed and vegetables; omnivores eat both meat and vegetables. Because we are talking about general categories there may be individuals in a species such that one is a carnivore and another is an omnivore. For example, the Yellow Watchman Goby is a meat eater while the Rainford Goby eats meat and filamentous algae.

Common Names and Scientific Names

You will find that many fish have multiple names, both common and scientific names are used in the industry. Some fish have multiple common names. The Pacific Blue Tang, for example, is also called Hippo Tang, Regal Tang and Yellow Tail Tang. The scientific name of this tang is Paracanthurus hepatus.

Reef Safe Fish

Assessor

Yellow Assessor (Assessor flavissimus) and Blue Assessor (Assessor macneilli)

Yellow Assessor

Assessors are colorful, hardy and safe to mix with corals and invertebrates. Many aquarium stores offer captive-hatched and raised Assessors. The two most common species are simply named Yellow and Blue Assessors. As their names imply, one is a bright yellow (with red along the edge of the fins) and the other is a beautiful grayish blue.

Assessors are territorial towards their own species and it is best to have just one per tank. Large aquariums with plenty of caves and overhangs can have two or more assessors, if they are added at the same time. These fish grow to only three inches long and are not aggressive towards other species. They do best in aquariums with non-aggressive fish.

In the wild and usually in a mini reef aquarium, Assessors are found in caves and overhangs, often swimming upside down. You will probably notice their tendency to stay close to caves, especially if there are a lot of other fish in the aquarium.

Assessors are carnivores which readily eat frozen meaty foods. Captive-raised fish will eat dry foods right away.

Angelfish - Dwarf

Coral Beauty Angelfish (Centropyge bispinosa), Flame Angelfish (Centropyge loriculus), Flameback Angelfish (African) (Centropyge acanthops), Pygmy (Cherub) Angelfish (Centropyge argi), Red Stripe Angelfish (Centropyge eibli) and Venustus Angelfish (Sumireyakko venustus)

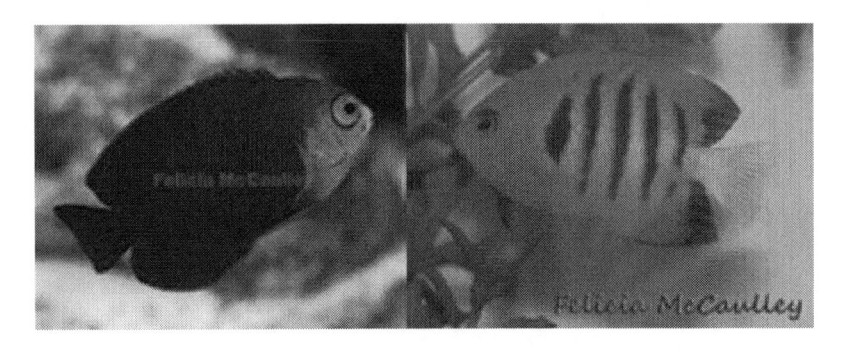

Pygmy and Flame Angelfish

Dwarf Angelfish are one of the most popular reef fish available. Most have bright vivid colors and live long, beautiful lives in established aquariums. Angelfish can be easily distinguished from other species by a sharp spine located at the lower front of the gill cover; this is their weapon for protection or to attack other fish.

Depending on the species, dwarf Angelfish grow to three to six inches in length. These fish are generally compatible with other species like tangs, Gobies, Wrasses, etc, but are usually aggressive towards each other. Dwarf angels tend to be territorial, and for this reason it is best to keep only one in a small aquarium. In larger aquariums, dwarf Angelfish of different sizes can live together. Try to add juvenile Angelfish at the same time to your aquarium so that they grow and change together.

To feel secure, Angelfish like lots of caves and places to hide.

Angelfish spend most of their day picking or nipping at algae and detritus on sand, rocks, corals, aquarium glass, etc. Dwarf angels are omnivorous and within a short time after being added to an aquarium will eat almost any food offered. Feed them a variety of foods to create a balanced diet of meats and algae.

There can be a downside to Angelfish in a reef: some dwarf angels will eat (nip) mucous produced by the corals and clams, rather than the flesh itself. If corals are healthy this nipping may not be a problem, but nipping may cause certain corals to stay retracted. If a coral remains retracted, and no longer opens, part of, or even the entire coral may die. Sometimes just moving a coral to a different location will cause the angel to leave it alone. Tridacna clams can also be harassed to death by a persistent nibbler. Retracting its fleshy mantle tissue repeatedly can exhaust a clam and even lead to death.

This said, a dwarf Angelfish generally makes a beautiful addition to a mini reef. For best success, keep it (them) well fed and choose your Angelfish wisely, keeping in mind that once a fish is added to a reef with live rock they can be very difficult to remove.

CAUTION: Dwarf Angels have a sharp spine located at the lower front of the gill cover which can get caught in a fish net. To transport, herd these little fish into a plastic container.

Angelfish - Large

Bellus Angelfish (Genicanthus bellus), Lamarck's Angelfish (Genicanthus lamarck), Japanese Swallowtail Angelfish (Genicanthus melanospilos) and Watanabei Angelfish (Genicanthus watanabei)

Japanese Swallowtail (Female) and Bellus Angelfish (female)

There are a lot of large beautiful Angelfish that will thrive in an aquarium, but only a few are reef safe. Some of the best reef safe Angelfish are under the genus Genicanthus, also known as the swallowtail angels. Most of the Genicanthus Angelfish will typically mix safely with corals, shrimp, crabs and snails, etc. Rarely do these Angelfish feed on coral polyps, especially if kept well fed.

Another great attribute about the Genicanthus angels is that it is easy to distinguish the males from the females. This means that if your aquarium is large enough, you can add a pair of Angelfish. With some species, you can actually add a school of them! If your reef is small, a lone male or female will do well. Do a little research before choosing one of these angels since some can grow up to nine inches long. Even though some Angelfish grow large, they are all usually compatible with species such as tangs, Gobies, Wrasses, etc.

Just like all the Angelfish, Genicanthus have a sharp spine located on the lower front of the gill cover. They use this spine to protect themselves and to attack other fish. Keep your Angelfish happy and secure by creating plenty of caves and places for it/them to hide.

Also, to keep these Angelfish healthy feed them a variety of foods since they are omnivorous. In the wild, Genicanthus eat plankton, algae, and some species eat sponge. For these angels, there are several prepared frozen foods available.

CAUTION: Angels have a sharp spine located at the lower front of the gill cover which can get caught in a fish net. To transport, herd these little fish into a plastic container.

Anthias

Bartlett's Anthias (Pseudanthias bartlettorum), Dispar Anthias (Pseudanthias dispar), Lyretail Anthias (Pseudanthias squamipinnis), Randall's Anthias (Pseudanthias randalli) and Resplendent Anthias (Pseudanthias pulcherrimus)

Lyretail Anthias (male and female)

Anthias are generally safe to keep with corals and invertebrates. Their striking colors also draw many reef hobbyists to purchase them. These fish have colors that vary with each species. One popular Anthias has a purple body with a bright yellow stripe, another has a solid orange body and yet another has a red head, bright orange body and a yellow tail. You can see why hobbyists want these beautiful fish for their mini reefs.

Anthias are found in large schools in the wild, so some hobbyists try to duplicate nature and attempt to keep small schools in their reef tank. This can be quite a challenge since there are many factors that influence results such as the size of the aquarium, the choice of species and even the distribution of males and females within the group. A school of Anthias is in reality a very complex system, a system that can be difficult to mimic in an aquarium. For most hobbyists, it is best to keep only one Anthias of a given species in a reef.

Anthias are very diverse among species, some are easy to keep and are peaceful and others are semi-aggressive and difficult to keep. Most Anthias will get along with other tank mates but they can often be aggressive towards their own species. The majority of Anthias will grow to be three to five inches in length; a few species can grow quite large - up to eight inches.

In the wild, Anthias eat zooplankton throughout the day. In a home aquarium these fish do best on a meaty diet, and are best fed two to three times a day. If feeding your fish once a day is your plan, it is wise to choose different fish.

Basslet

Chalk Bass (Serranus tortugarum), Royal Gramma Basslet (Gramma loreto), Swalesi Basslet (Liopropoma swalesi) and Swissguard Basslet (Liopropoma rubre)

Royal Gramma and Chalk Bass

Basslets are another popular choice for reef hobbyists since they stay small, are very hardy, are easy to care for and are inexpensive (compared to many saltwater fish.) Several species of Basslets have bright colors. Royal Grammas, for instance, are a magnificent purple on the front part of their body with a brilliant yellow back portion.

Most Basslets remain small, growing to only about two to three inches long. For protection in the wild, Basslets live in and around rocky areas. In the home aquarium, make sure you have lots of caves and hiding places so they will feel secure.

Since many Basslets are territorial they are best when kept only one per aquarium. Chalk Basslets are an exception to this rule as they are not territorial. If your aquarium is large and you add several at the same time, they should do well together.

Basslets are carnivores, require a high protein diet, and will readily eat almost any frozen fish food. They are safe with corals but may eat small ornamental crustaceans; small shrimp, snails and crabs might be at risk to these otherwise adorable fish.

Blennies

Barnacle Blenny (Acanthemblemaria macrospilus), Bicolor Blenny (Ecsenius bicolor), Black Combtooth Blenny (Ecsenius namiyei), Canary Blenny (Meiacanthus oualanensis), Black Sailfin Blenny (Atrosalarias fuscus), Ember Blenny (Cirripectes stigmaticus), Forktail Blenny (Meiacanthus atrodorsalis), Green Canary Blenny (Meiacanthus tongaensis), Harptail Blenny (Meiacanthus mossambicus), Horseface Blenny (Ophioblennius atlanticus), Midas Blenny (Ecsenius midas), Lawnmower Blenny (Salarias fasciatus), Starry Blenny (Salarias ramosus) and Striped Blenny (Meiacanthus grammistes)

Bicolor and Lawnmower Blenny

Blennies are a large diverse family with only a few relatively reef safe species as listed above. Most Blennies are hardy, easy to care for and do well in an aquarium.

Blennies are entertaining and fun to watch. Most Blennies will prop themselves up on their pectoral fins and watch everything that goes on around them. Most Blennies will spend much time near or on the bottom of the aquarium. Blennies are very curious and nervous; if startled they quickly dart to safety in a rock, crevice or cave.

There are a few brilliant yellow Blennies, but the majority of species are plain, dull colors. Many will grow to about three inches long while others can grow over six inches in length. Blennies are territorial towards members of their own species so it is ideal to keep just one of any particular species in an aquarium.

Some Blennies are herbivores, others carnivores, and still others are omnivorous. Many will graze on microalgae growing on the rocks and sand. Unfortunately, some Blennies, such as bicolor, algae or lawnmower and horse face Blennies may nip at stony coral polyps and clam mantles. Others, like Barnacle Blennies, are totally reef safe. Barnacle Blennies, as the name might imply, are adorable miniature fish whose maximum length of two inches makes it easy for them to slide into tiny holes in the live rock and call them home. At feeding time, a barnacle blenny darts out of its hole at lightning speed, grabs a piece of food and darts back in to its home. If you blink, you will miss it!

Since Blennies are very diverse, you need to research your favorite blenny before going out and buying it.

Cardinalfish

Five-Lined Cardinalfish (Cheilodipterus quinquelineatus), Flame Cardinal (Apogon spp.), Banggai Cardinalfish (Pterapogon kauderni), Longspine Cardinalfish (Zoramia leptacantha), Orbic Cardinalfish (Sphaeramia orbicularis), Pajama Cardinalfish (Sphaeramia nematoptera) and Yellowstriped Cardinalfish (Ostorhinchus cyanosoma)

Banggai and Pajama Cardinalfish

Cardinalfish are yet another popular reef fish that are easy to care for. Cardinalfish are easy to distinguish by the distinctive two separate dorsal fins on their backs. Their large eyes are common in nocturnal fish. Since Cardinalfish are nocturnal you may see them spending the day in caves and other shaded areas in your live rock and find them more active at night. As a group they stay small; most species are less than four inches long.

Peaceful towards their tank mates, many species of Cardinalfish such as Longspine Cardinalfish do well in schools, while others, like Flame Cardinal, prefer to be in pairs.

Cardinalfish are carnivores and most will readily eat a varied diet.

Banggai, Pajama and Longspine Cardinalfish are bred in captivity. An odd fact about Cardinalfish is that a male will hold fertilized eggs in his mouth for protection. In about a week the eggs will hatch. It is possible for baby Cardinalfish to survive in hobbyists' reef aquariums as long as they are not eaten by tank mates.

Chromis

Blue Reef Chromis (Chromis cyaneus), Blue Green Chromis (Chromis viridis), Sunshine Chromis (Chromis insolata) and Yellow Chromis (Chromis analis)

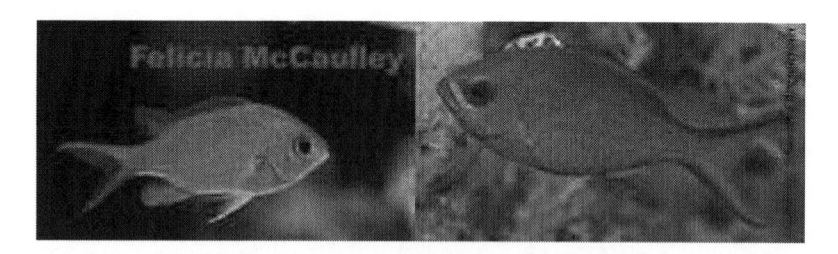

Blue Green and Blue Reef Chromis

Chromis are peaceful fish, ideal for a reef for those who prefer schooling fish. Chromis look similar to damsel fish but they definitely do not have the aggressive bullying behavior.

Most Chromis stay out in the open usually swimming in the upper portion of an aquarium. They prefer to be in schools which apparently appeal to their sense of security. If something scares them they will disperse and dash inside the rock work.

Most Chromis grow to three inches long, but Blue Reef Chromis grow to about five inches long. The peaceful nature of Chromis makes them easy to mix with nonaggressive fish, although you may see them quarreling among themselves. Chromis are safe with corals and invertebrates.

Chromis are carnivorous and will readily eat any food that is put in the aquarium.

Clownfish

Clarkii Clownfish (Amphiprion clarkii), Maroon Clownfish (Premnas biaculeatus), Ocellaris Clownfish (Amphiprion ocellaris), Orange Skunk Clownfish (Amphiprion sandaracinos), Pink Skunk Clownfish (Amphiprion perideraion), Tomato Clownfish (Amphiprion frenatus) and True Percula Clownfish (Amphiprion percula)

Ocellaris and Pink Skunk Clownfish

Snowflake and Black Ocellaris Clownfish

Clownfish - especially since the movie "Finding Nemo" - are the most recognized and commonly kept of all saltwater fish. The movie stars the top-selling Ocellaris Clownfish with a strikingly deep-orange body and bright white stripes. Clownfish can be pink, yellow, black, maroon or red, and most have white stripes. They are hardy and easy to keep, making them great starter fish for a beginning hobbyist. Many Clownfish are hatched and raised in captivity. These fish are generally hardier than wild caught and more easily assimilate into new aquariums than their wild-caught counterparts.

Clownfish are generally excellent additions to a living reef although some Clownfish species become very aggressive towards their tank mates as they mature. Another possible downside to housing Clownfish in a reef aquarium is that occasionally one of these magnificent creatures will settle on using the polyps of a coral to burrow into when no sea anemone is present. A Clownfish residing in live coral may cause its coral to keep its polyps partially or completely retracted. Therefore the coral may starve.

Skunk Clownfish in Red Carpet Anemone

Many people have seen pictures of Clownfish hiding or playing in the tentacles of a sea anemone. While Clownfish use anemones for protection in the wild, they can live well in a reef aquarium with or without an anemone.

Sea anemones have drawbacks of which a reef-keeper should be aware. When you place a sea anemone in the very spot that it looks great, you have little guarantee that it will stay put! Anemones are more mobile than one would think, and will move wherever they want, often ending up in a place that is hard to see. They may even stick to the glass of the aquarium! Another challenge to housing an anemone is that they can sting and kill corals. For this reason alone, most reef hobbyists choose to keep just a Clownfish or two without an anemone.

Clownfish are protandrous hermaphrodites, meaning that these fish are born male and turn into females. When adding two Clownfish to an aquarium, choose two different-sized fish. The larger, more dominant fish will slowly develop into a female if it is not already. The female will be more aggressive than the male, attacking or chasing off other fish that wander into their territory.

Most Clownfish do best when kept alone or in pairs. A pair can aggressively protect their territory. Only add one species of Clownfish to your aquarium. If you add different species in the same aquarium the most aggressive Clownfish can kill off less dominant Clownfish.

Most Clownfish will grow to about three inches while some species can grow up to seven inches in length.

Clownfish are generally hardy eaters and the first ones to the dinner table. Clownfish are omnivorous and will eat almost any saltwater food that hits the water.

Damselfish

Yellowtail Damselfish (Chrysiptera parasema), Blue Damselfish (Chrysiptera cyanea), Talbot's Damselfish (Chrysiptera talboti), Azure Damselfish (Chrysiptera hemicyanea) and Yellow Damselfish (Amblyglyphidodon aureus)

Azure and Yellowtail Damselfish

Damselfish are very popular among beginning hobbyists because of their bright colors and inexpensive price. Unfortunately, damsel fish are territorial and constantly chase each other. This constant bullying behavior can take away the enjoyment and calming effect of watching a living reef.

If you prefer a passive reef it is best to skip Damselfish and choose calm, peaceful, schooling Chromis. That said, Damselfish are extremely hardy and easy to keep. Most become very territorial as they mature and often exhibit aggressive behavior towards tank mates and new fish. It is vital to have an abundance of caves and crevices for these fish to claim. Remember that adding fish to the reef is the easy part; trying to catch a fish can be VERY difficult and the entire reef may have to be dismantled. Choose carefully before introducing any fish!

Yellowtail Damselfish are among the least aggressive. They are beautiful, with their bright blue bodies and bright yellow tails. They are usually peaceful towards tank mates, although may quarrel among themselves.

Damselfish are active swimmers and most of the Damsels listed above will grow up to three inches long.

Damsels are omnivores, are not picky and will eagerly eat either frozen or dry foods. They are safe to keep with corals and invertebrates.

Dartfish

Blue Gudgeon (Ptereleotris heteroptera), Firefish (Nemateleotris magnifica), Purple Firefish (Nemateleotris decora), Scissortail (Ptereleotris evides) and Zebra Barred (Ptereleotris zebra)

NOTE: For this discussion Dartfish are separated by Genus into two sections.

Dartfish (Genus Ptereleotris)

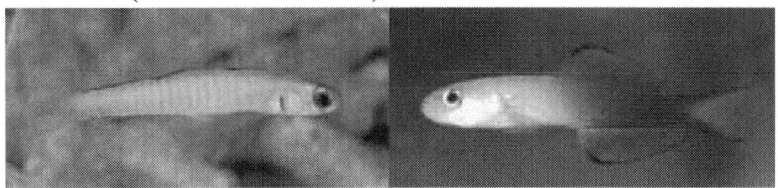

Zebra Barred and Scissortail

Dartfish are a great group of fish for mini reefs. These elongated fish are hardy, peaceful and easy to care for and safe to mix with corals and invertebrates.

Dartfish can be kept singularly or in pairs, however they do best as a group of a single species. The group usually hangs around the middle of the aquarium and needs lots of caves and crevices to make a hasty retreat when frightened. Species like the Blue Gudgeon will make a burrow in the sand and dart into their burrow for protection.

Depending on the species, some can grow to a maximum of four inches while others can grow up to five and half inches long. Keep these peaceful fish with other nonaggressive fish.

Their elongated body allows them to be great jumpers, so be sure your aquarium has an enclosed lid or you'll find them dried up on your floor!

Dartfish are carnivores and will eat both frozen and dry meaty foods. They stay out in the open always on the lookout for food. Even though they are meat eaters, they are safe to mix with invertebrates and corals.

Firefish (Genus Nemateleotris spp.)

Firefish and Purple Firefish

Firefish are hardy, peaceful, easy to keep and safe with corals and invertebrates. These delicate looking fish are elongated, very colorful and have a distinctive long back fin (dorsal ray.)

These fish need caves and crevices to feel secure. When threatened they will shoot into the live rock. Also when frightened they can jump out of the aquarium and plunge to their death. An enclosed top is a must for this quick moving escape artist!

Firefish grow to a length of two and half or three inches long depending on the species. It is best to keep one fish or a male and female. If adding more than two Firefish, one will quickly become dominant over the others and begin bullying and nipping fins. This can ultimately lead to death for the less aggressive fish.

Dottyback

Bicolor Dottyback (Pictichromis paccagnellae), Indigo Dottyback (Pseudochromis fridmani x sankeyi), Neon Dottyback (Pseudochromis aldabraensis), Orchid Dottyback (Pseudochromis fridmani), Purple Stripe Dottyback (Pseudochromis diadema), Springeri Dottyback (Pseudochromis springerii) and Sunrise Dottyback (Pseudochromis flavivertex)

Orchid Dottyback

Several Dottyback species have bright striking purple and/or intense yellow colors. Most stay small and tank-raised Dottybacks are very hardy.

Dottybacks need lots of caves and crevices so that they can choose their hiding place as many enjoy swimming in and out of rocks. Dottybacks will defend their hiding place from intruders. Though smaller Dottybacks only grow to about three inches long they are able defend their territories against much larger fish. The Indigo Dottyback is an exception; it has a peaceful demeanor. The other extreme is the Royal Dottyback which can be very aggressive towards other tank mates.

In general, keep only one Dottyback in an aquarium as they are aggressive towards their own species. It is possible to keep several Dottybacks in large aquariums with lots of rock work.

Some Dottybacks are free swimmers while other will not venture far from their rock crevice or cave. When startled, they will dart back to their hiding place. Many species are tank-raised and will adjust quickly to a reef aquarium.

Dottybacks are carnivores; tank-raised varieties will readily eat frozen or dry foods. They also eat any worms and other tiny critters they may find in the aquarium. Several species are beneficial to reefs because they will consume dreaded bristle worms. Dottybacks are safe with corals but may eat small invertebrates; they can harass and are known to kill shrimp.

Gobies

Bluespotted Watchman Goby (Cryptocentrus pavoninoides), Clown Goby (Gobiodon citrinus), Clown Goby, Green (Gobiodon atrangulatus), Clown Goby, Yellow (Gobiodon okinawae), Court Jester Goby (Amblygobius rainfordi), Diagonal Bar Prawn Goby (Amblyeleotris diagonalis), Diamond Watchman Goby (Valenciennea puellaris), Engineer Goby (Pholidichthys leucotaenia), Hector's Goby (Amblygobius hectori), Hi Fin Red Banded Goby (Stonogobiops nematodes), Neon Goby (Elacatinus oceanops), Orange Spotted Goby (Amblyeleotris guttata), Orange Stripe Prawn Goby (Amblyeleotris randalli), Pink Spotted Watchman Goby(Cryptocentrus leptocephalus), Pinkbar Goby (Amblyeleotris aurora), Red Head Goby (Elacatinus puncticulatus), Sleeper Banded Goby (Amblygobius phalaena), Sleeper Gold Head Goby (Valenciennea strigata), Tiger Watchman Goby (Valenciennea wardii), Two Spot Goby (Signigobius biocellatus), Wheeler's Shrimp Goby (Amblyeleotris wheeleri), Yasha White Ray Shrimp Goby (Stonogobiops yasha) and Yellow Watchman Goby (Cryptocentrus cinctus)

Yellow Clown and Orange Stripe Prawn Goby

High Fin Red Banded and Diamond Goby

Gobies are a huge family comprising over 2000 different species of fish. Therefore the information discussed here will be very general and based on the species listed above. Many gobies will grow to one and a half to around six inches long. Most are easy to keep and peaceful. Nearly all Gobies (except Sleeper Gobies) have a pelvic sucking disc, which in the ocean allows them to attach to rocks and not get swept away by the current. In the reef, they will either perch on rocks with their disc and may even attach themselves to the aquarium glass.

Most Gobies stay in the lower portion of the aquarium and some dig burrows in the sand. The rockwork provides numerous spots for Gobies to hide and feel comfortable. Most Gobies are relatively small with an elongated body enabling them to be good jumpers. Make sure you have an enclosed top on your aquarium.

One of the most fascinating characteristics about some Gobies is their symbiotic relationship with pistol shrimp. A shrimp and Goby will live together in a burrow which the shrimp excavated. The shrimp will maintain the burrow while the Goby stands guard near the entrance. When a predator comes near, the Goby alerts the shrimp. They both will hide in the burrow until the danger is gone. They will also sleep together in their burrow.

Yasha White Ray Shrimp Goby and Candy Stripe Pistol Shrimp

A few Gobies that mix with pistol shrimps are Hi Fin Red Banded Gobies, Yasha White Ray Shrimp Gobies and Yellow Watchman Gobies. A few pistol shrimps which make great companions are Tiger Snapping, Snapping, and Red Banded Shrimp.

Hogfish
Yellow Candy Hogfish (Bodianus bimaculatus)

Candy Hogfish (most often available in bright yellow)

Candy Hogfish stay small and are safe with corals but may either eat or harass invertebrates. They are an eye-catching bright yellow with light red horizontal stripes along the body.

This hogfish fish stays tiny, growing to a maximum length of approximately four inches. Young fish are peaceful; as they age they may become semi-aggressive towards tank mates. It is best to only keep one Candy Hogfish in an aquarium. Their elongated bodies make them excellent jumpers and make it necessary to keep the aquarium completely enclosed.

Candy Hogfish are carnivores and, as mentioned, can harass or eat shrimp and other invertebrates but are safe with corals.

Jawfish

Black Cap (Opistognathus randalli), Blue Dot (Opistognathus rosenblatti), Dusky (Opistognathus whitehursti), Pearly (Opistognathus aurifrons) , Tiger (Opistognathus sp.) and Yellowhead (Opistognathus aurifrons)

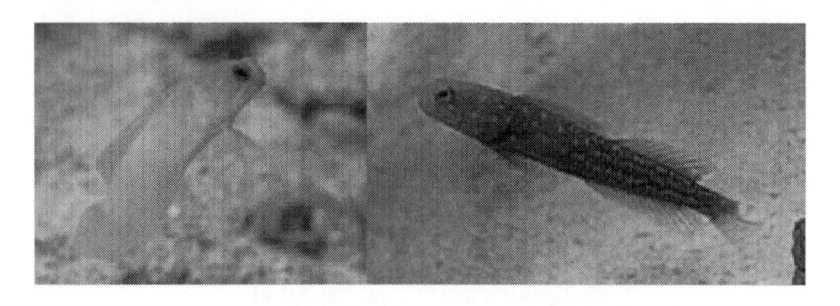

Pearly and Blue Dot Jawfish

Jawfish are peaceful and fun to watch as they build and take care of their home. Jawfish are easy to recognize with their elongated body, long continuous fin on top and under their bodies, a huge mouth, and very large eyes. Their huge mouth is used to dig their home.

Jawfish create their homes by digging a burrow in the sand. They literally take mouthfuls of sand and spit it out somewhere else in the aquarium. Corals close by the burrow can be covered in expelled sand. They will continue moving the sand until a tunnel is created. The Jawfish will spend much time in his burrow with just his head peeking out. If a fish swims near the burrow, the Jawfish will try to chase it away.

To construct the burrow the Jawfish needs various size sand, rubble and small shells or pieces of shells. Since Jawfish can dig under the rockwork it is best to stack the rock in the aquarium before adding the sand so that the Jawfish cannot burrow under the rockwork and cause the rocks to tumble.

Jawfish, depending on species, will grow to three and a half to four inches in length. Again, depending on the species, you can keep more than one in an aquarium. When startled, Jawfish will either dart back to their burrow or they may jump out of the aquarium. Keep the top of your aquarium covered.

Jawfish are carnivores. During feeding time, they will dart in and out of their burrow. Some species will eat invertebrates but all are safe with corals.

Mandarin

Green Mandarin (Synchiropus splendidus), Spotted Mandarin (Synchiropus picturatus) and Red Mandarin (Synchiropus cf. splendidus)

Green Mandarin

Green and Red Mandarins are some of the most beautiful, colorful fish with unique patterns you will find in the ocean. Mandarins make excellent reef fish since they are safe to keep with corals and invertebrates.

These fish are fun to watch as they scoot around the sand and live rock looking for food. Wild-caught Mandarins are difficult to keep alive long-term in an aquarium because they forage for amphipods and copepods which may not be as abundant in a home reef aquarium as they are in the ocean. In established reefs, and with a refugium, it is possible for wild-caught Mandarins to find enough food; it is also possible to supplement these foods with commercial packaged amphipods and copepods. This can be a lot of work for a hobbyist (continually adding live foods) and, sadly, most wild-caught

Mandarins starve to death over time. Choosing tank-raised Mandarins can eliminate this difficulty and most will devour a variety of frozen and dry foods.

Mandarins are fun to watch and will live with a variety of nonaggressive saltwater fish. They stay small, grow to three and a half to four inches long, and can be found in three colors, each with unique patterns. Males are easy to recognize by their long first dorsal spine. Do not keep two males together - they will fight!

CAUTION: Mandarins have a sharp spine on their cheeks which can get caught in a fish net. To transport, herd these little fish into a plastic container.

Tang

Blonde Naso Tang (Naso elegans), Blue Tang (Paracanthurus hepatus), Bristletooth Tomini Tang (Ctenochaetus tominiensis), Chevron Tang (Ctenochaetus hawaiiensis), Convict Tang (Acanthurus triostegus), Desjardini (Zebrasoma desjardini), Kole Yellow Eye Tang (Ctenochaetus strigosus), Lieutenant Tang (Acanthurus tennenti), Orangeshoulder Tang (Acanthurus olivaceous), Naso Tang (Naso lituratus), Powder Blue Tang (Acanthurus leucosternon), Purple Tang (Zebrasoma xanthurum), Sailfin Tang (Zebrasoma veliferum), Scopas Tang (Zebrasoma scopas), Vlamingii Tang (Naso vlamingii), Whitecheek Tang (Acanthurus nigricans) and Hawaiian Yellow Tang (Zebrasoma flavescens)

Powder Blue and Yellow Tang

Sailfin and Pacific Blue Tang

Tangs are so popular that almost every reef has at least one and it is usually the largest fish in the aquarium. Tangs are often called surgeonfish, a name derived from the scalpel-like spines on both sides of their bodies just before their tail. These spines are an instrument of defense to protect themselves and their territories.

Tangs can aggressively defend their territory against fish with similar body shapes and colors. Generally keep one Tang per tank. Larger aquariums can keep multiple Tangs as long as they have different shapes, colors and sizes. For instance, an elongated Pacific Blue Tang will usually live well in an aquarium with the more rounded Yellow Tang. It is also possible to keep schools of the same species of Tangs in large aquariums if they are introduced into the aquarium at the same time.

One of the most popular Tangs is the Blue Tang. Like Nemo the clownfish, this fish became famous as Dory in the movie Finding Nemo. This movie created such an interest in the Blue Tang that it became one of the most sought after fish in aquarium stores. Even today, long after the movie's popularity peaked, Blue Tangs remain one of the bestselling species of fish available.

Most adult Tangs require an aquarium of at least 75 gallons. Blue Tangs are both beautiful and hardy, but can grow quite large. It is not unusual to find Blue Tangs up to a foot long in the ocean; Vlamingii Tangs often grow to two feet long in the wild! The smallest Tang in our list above is the Bristletooth Tomini Tang, which grows to six inches long. Since Tangs are found in such a huge range of sizes, research your favorite species before making a purchase to make sure the tang you choose will not outgrow your aquarium.

Tangs are active swimmers so always ensure the rock is stacked to provide plenty of holes and spaces for them to swim. Many Tangs spend their days grazing the live rock looking for algae. Tangs are herbivores and generally good eaters. Feed them a diet rich in algae and other vegetables. Supplement their diet by feeding Nori algae sheets once or twice a week.

There are a few Tangs, such as Chevron, Convict, Bristletooth Tomini, Whitecheek and Hawaiian Yellow, which are safe with both corals and invertebrates.

Wrasse

Carpenter's Flasher Wrasse (Paracheilinus carpenteri), Eightline Wrasse (Pseudocheilinus octotaenia), Exquisite Fairy Wrasse (Cirrhilabrus exquisitus), Labout's Fairy Wrasse (Cirrhilabrus laboutei), Lineatus Fairy Wrasse (Cirrhilabrus lineatus), Longfin Fairy Wrasse (Cirrhilabrus rubriventralis), Lubbock's Fairy Wrasse (Cirrhilabrus lubbocki), McCosker's Flasher Wrasse (Paracheilinus mccoskeri), Mystery Wrasse (Pseudocheilinus ocellatus), Pink Margin Fairy Wrasse (Cirrhilabrus rubrimarginatus), Red Velvet Fairy Wrasse (Cirrhilabrus rubrisquamis), Scott's Fairy Wrasse (Cirrhilabrus scottorum), Six Line Wrasse (Pseudocheilinus hexataenia), Solorensis Fairy Wrasse (Cirrhilabrus solorensis), Yellow Banded Possum Wrasse (Wetmorella nigropinnata), Whip Fin Fairy Wrasse (Cirrhilabrus filamentosus) and White Banded Possum Wrasse (Wetmorella albofasciata)

The Wrasse family is huge and offers some amazing gems for our reef aquariums. Wrasses are very diverse, therefore they are divided up into a number of different Genus. Since Wrasses from the same Genus have similar requirements we will discuss them by Genus. We will only discuss the best and safest Genus for our reef aquariums.

Felicia Mccaulley

Longfin Fairy Wrasse

Wrasses of the Genus Cirrhilabrus are called Fairy Wrasses. These are typically very active, peaceful fish; male Fairy Wrasses have truly amazing colors. Males are much more colorful than the females. Once acclimated to a reef, they will readily eat meaty foods. A Fairy Wrasse will make a mucus cocoon to protect it while sleeping among the rockwork. A couple of great choices are Solorensis Fairy Wrasse and Labout's Fairy Wrasse; both are hardy, colorful and safe with corals and invertebrates.

McCosker's Flasher Wrasse

Wrasses of the Genus Paracheilinus are called Flasher Wrasses. The name comes from the way a male Wrasse "flashes" when courting or protecting its territory. While flashing, he spreads out his top fin and tail fin as blood rushes to the scales creating a beautiful colorful display. The Flashers have similar characteristics to the Fairy Wrasses except they are smaller. Flashers also have hearty appetites and eat meaty foods. Males are more colorful than the females. The Flasher Wrasse will also create a mucus cocoon when it sleeps among the rockwork.

Six Line Wrasse

Wrasses of the Genus Pseudocheilinus are called Lined Wrasses. Popular members of this group are the four and six line Wrasses. These fish are very hardy and stay small. Lined Wrasses spend their time searching out and eating flatworms and other pests in reef aquariums. The downside is that, when mature, they usually become pugnacious and bully new tank mates as well as other Wrasses. The Lined Wrasse will also create a mucus cocoon when it sleeps among the rockwork.

Yellow Banded Possum Wrasse

Wrasses of the Genus Wetmorella are called Possum Wrasses. These Wrasses are great for small reef aquariums, growing only to two and a half inches long. They are very hardy and easy to care for. A Yellow-Banded Possum Wrasse is a peaceful, secretive little fish which hides in the rock work. They are safe with corals and invertebrates.

There are a few general requirements for all of these reef safe Wrasses. Tank mates of reef safe Wrasses should be relatively peaceful fish. Wrasses are good jumpers and need an enclosed top on the aquarium. Since Wrasses are very active, they should be fed a meaty diet several times a day. All the above Wrasses are safe with corals. Invertebrates may become food for many of the Wrasses with exception of the Possum Wrasses.

There are a lot of reef safe Wrasses and most have different requirements. Before buying a Wrasse by its exotic beauty alone, make sure it will thrive in your aquarium.

FREE BONUS: Claim your FREE copy of " Livestock Tracking form and more" at http://9nl.be/FreeReefBonuses

Bringing Your New Fish Home

Now that you have purchased your fish, you want to keep them happy and healthy. Your fish will be sealed in a water and air-filled plastic bag with rubber bands or clasps holding the top closed. The parameters in the fish transportation bag (pH, salinity, temperature, etc.) may be different from your aquarium. New fish will do best if they are slowly acclimated to their new environment.

There are three methods to introduce your new fish into your saltwater aquarium and the method you choose is based on how long and how many fish were carried in their transportation bag. The longer the fish is left in the bag, the more stress it will endure. Stress can be caused by temperature change, rough handling, low oxygen levels and toxin build up in the water. Fish excrete toxic ammonia through their gills as well as in their waste and urine. Inside a closed fish bag an interesting thing can occur: over time, pH drops converting toxic ammonia to a less toxic ammonium. When the fish bag is opened, CO_2 (which is acid) escapes, the pH rises, and ammonium converts back into toxic ammonia.

One popular acclimation method used by many hobbyists is to place the water from the fish bag, along with the new fish, in a bucket. Using airline tubing, they will allow water from their aquarium to slowly drip into this bucket. The challenge with this method is that if the fish has been in the shipping bag for more than a couple of hours, a sizeable amount of ammonia and ammonium will have accumulated. Since the pH of a saltwater aquarium is typically above 8.0, while this water slowly drips into the bucket, the low pH in the bucket water rises. Research has found that ammonium is not readily taken into a fish's body, but ammonia easily passes through the fishes gills into the bloodstream. Then the fish's body converts this ammonia to ammonium. Inside the body ammonium causes damage affecting the central nervous system which manifests symptoms of fish darting and sinking.

If you still prefer to drip acclimate your fish which have been in their shipping water for long periods of time, use an ammonia binding agent which are readily available from several aquarium manufacturers. Ammonia binding agents are used for treating municipal water containing chloramines. Prime, by Seachem, is one product that claims to bind ammonia.

There are many variables to take in to account when choosing a method to acclimate new fish, including the number of fish that were put in a single transportation bag, the amount of water that was added to the bag, the size of the fish compared to the size of the bag and even when the fish ate its last meal can make it tricky to judge amounts of accumulated waste in a fish bag.

The most common methods of acclimation follow.

Methods to introducing fish to an aquarium:

Acclimation Method One

1. Turn aquarium lights off while floating the fish.

2. Float the sealed bag with the fish inside on top of the aquarium water for 15 - 30 minutes. The salesperson should have filled at least half the bag with air, enabling the bag to float in your aquarium. Floating the fish bag on the surface of the aquarium allows the water in the bag to gradually change to the same temperature as the aquarium water.

3. Use a thermometer to ensure the temperature of the water in the fish bags is the same as the aquarium water.

4. Release the fish into the aquarium. To accomplish this, you can pinch the end of the bag and pour all of the water into a bucket, then pour the fish into the aquarium; OR pour the fish into a net over a sink or bucket to catch the water from the bag, then release the fish into the aquarium. The key here is to keep store water from entering your aquarium. Caution: Some fish such as angels and mandarins have spines which can get caught in a net.

TIP: Water from a fish store could contain copper or other medications! Do not add water from a fish bag to your aquarium!

Acclimation Method Two

1. Turn aquarium lights off.

2. Float sealed bag with the fish inside in the top of your aquarium or, if you prefer, in your sump for 15 minutes. The salesperson should have filled at least half the bag with air, enabling it to float in your aquarium. Floating the fish bag on the surface of the

aquarium allows the water in the bag to gradually change to the same temperature as the water in the aquarium.

3. Open the bag and roll down the sides to create an air pocket, which will allow the bag to continue to float.

4. Slowly add some water from your aquarium to the bag (about a 1/3 of the bag volume)

5. After 10 minutes, repeat step 4. Do this two more times.

6. Release the fish into the aquarium. To release the fish you can pinch the end of the bag and pour all of the water into a bucket, then pour the fish into the aquarium; OR pour the fish into a net and then release the fish into the aquarium. The key here is to keep store water from entering your aquarium. Caution: Fish such as angels and mandarins have spines which can get caught in a net.

Acclimation Method Three

1. Turn off the aquarium light to avoid stressing the fish.

2. Float the sealed bag with the fish in the top of the aquarium or sump for 15 to 30 minutes. The salesperson should have filled at least half the bag with air, enabling the bag to float in your aquarium. This allows the water in the bag to gradually change to the same temperature as the aquarium water.

3. Put a clean nontoxic container or bucket in front of the aquarium. The number of fish and their sizes determine the size of the bucket. For two small fish (less than three inches each) a one gallon container will do.

NOTE: When acclimating a new fish make sure you keep it in a separate container from invertebrates and corals that you acclimate at the same time.

4. Once the temperature of the new fish water is the same as your aquarium, open the bag and pour the fish gently into the bucket. If there is not enough water to cover the fish, place something under one side of the bucket to raise the water level on the other side.

Fish released into bucket of water

5. Add an ammonia neutralizing product to the bucket of water with the fish. There are several products available at fish stores used to quickly neutralize ammonia.

6. Start a siphon to slowly drip water from your aquarium into the container. The siphon is a section of airline tubing, generally four to six feet long, with an adjustable valve on one end.

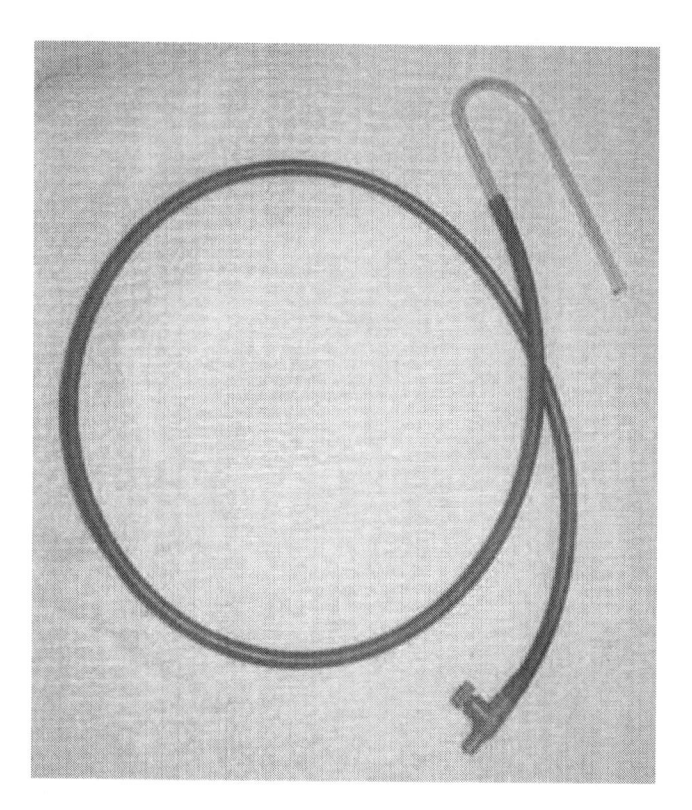

Drip line with plastic u-shape pipe to hang on rim of aquarium, airline tubing and valve

Place the end of the tubing without the valve in your aquarium and suck on the valve end to begin water flowing. Place the valve end into the bucket and slowly open and close it until the valve allows just two to four drops per second to drip through.

Water from aquarium slowly dripping into bucket

7. Cover the bucket to keep fish from jumping out and to keep it dark.

8. When the water in the bucket has doubled, dip out half of the water and discard it.

9. Let the water level double again.

10. Now, transfer the fish one at a time to the aquarium using a fish net or small plastic container. Caution: Some fish, like angelfish and mandarin fish have rays which can get caught in a net.

NOTE: This unhurried acclimation method will slowly raise the ph along with leveling out specific gravity and other water parameters. Remember; always acclimate in a shaded or dark area as fish are sensitive to sudden light changes.

11. Add premixed saltwater to the aquarium to replace water removed for acclimation.

Whichever acclimation method you chose, follow these tips as well:

TIPS: Feed a small amount of food to help distract the original inhabitants from picking on the new fish. Leave aquarium light off for a few hours to calm fish and keep them from harassing each other. When new fish enter the aquarium, you may see both territorial disputes and changes in the pecking order. These behaviors are both natural.

Once you decide on fish for your reef there are several books devoted to giving in-depth information about individual fish. These books can be found under Recommended Reading at the end of this guide.

Chapter 6

Invertebrates are Beneficial and Fun

Invertebrates are entertaining with their playful antics, daily routines and unique personalities. Snails, crabs, urchins, starfish, fan worms, shrimps and clams are all invertebrates; these animals do not have a backbone. Some of these invertebrates are beneficial for a reef aquarium because they consume unwanted algae, detritus (particles of organic material) and uneaten fish foods. Others are just fun to watch.

After your aquarium has cycled, the live rock should look clean. Organisms like plants, algae, bacteria, etc., begin covering the once pristine rock. As livestock is added and fed, waste levels begin to build; these levels are naturally reduced to nitrate, a food for algae. This nitrate, combined with intense reef lights, provides perfect conditions for algae to grow. There is actually a purpose for this unsightly algae - it helps reduce nitrate levels. The trick is to control algae, not eliminate it. We do this with a carefully selected balance of fish and invertebrates.

In this section we will discuss different types of invertebrates and how they interact in a reef aquarium. Invertebrates are sold individually or in assortments called reef cleaners, cleaning packs or cleanup crews. These packages include snails, crabs, shrimp, etc.

If your rock is clean, it will take few invertebrates to keep it clean. Obviously, add more if your rocks have excessive algae growth or detritus build up. Invertebrates can be added at any time.

Invertebrates are very sensitive to rapid changes in water quality. Because of this, it is important to use a proven method to acclimate new invertebrates into your aquarium. (See Bringing Your New Invertebrates Home.) To keep water quality ideal and nitrate levels less than 10ppm, consistent partial water changes (see How to Care for a Reef) are necessary.

While there is an enormous selection of invertebrates available to hobbyists, we will limit out discussion to the safest and most beneficial ones for a mini reef aquarium.

Crabs

In order for a crab to grow it must periodically shed its exoskeleton (external skeleton) which supports and protects its body. An exoskeleton which has been shed has incredible detail and often looks like a dead crab lying on the sand. Before being alarmed, remove the remains and, if it is empty, you will find that it is simply an exoskeleton.

Hermit Crabs are different from true crabs as they do not make their own shells. Hermit crabs use empty snail shells to house and protect their bodies from predators. As they grow, they seek out larger shells so it is sensible to offer different sized empty shells in the aquarium. If a Hermit Crab does not find the right sized empty shell, it can drag a snail out of its shell killing it.

Blue Leg Reef Hermit Crabs (Calcinus tricolor)

Blue Leg Hermit Crab

Blue Leg Hermit Crabs are peaceful and excellent reef cleaners. Their legs are bright blue with a few red bands. While Blue Leg

Hermits stay small, their voracious appetite for nuisance algae, detritus and excess food makes them perfect reef scavengers. Only growing to an inch long allows this crab to squeeze into and clean tight spaces in the rockwork where other larger scavengers cannot reach. They will also sift through sand searching for food.

Blue Leg Hermit Crabs eat many types of algae including hair algae, film algae, cyanobacteria (red slime algae) and detritus. Their small size makes them a great addition to the cleanup crew. Add one Blue Leg Hermit for each five to ten gallons of aquarium water.

They are safe with corals. As the crab grows, keep various sized empty shells in aquarium; remember that it can pull small snails out of their shells.

Emerald Crab (Mithraculus sculptus)

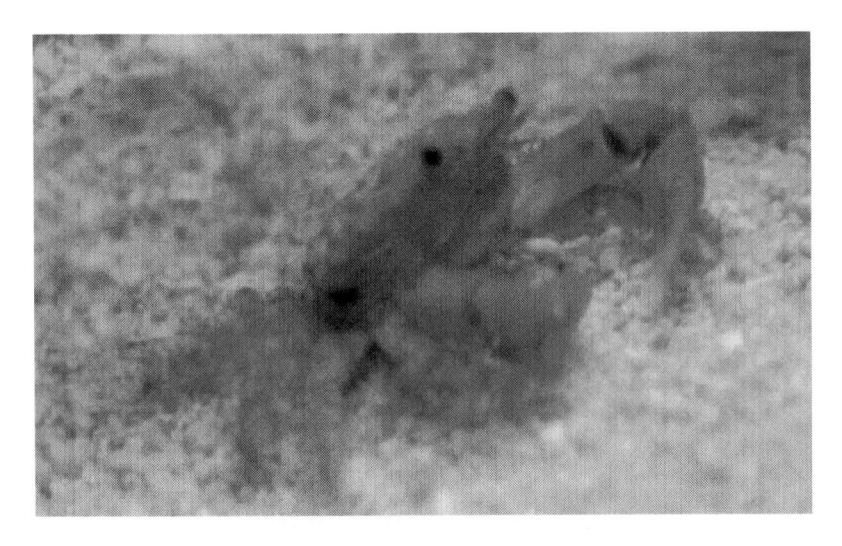

Emerald Crab

Emerald Crabs are green, with a flat shaped body, hairy legs and large claws. They use their claws to scrape and eat micro and macro algae (including bubble algae) off the rock.

Even though Emerald Crabs are nocturnal, once they are used to their new environment they will be out during the day scouring rocks for food. As long as an Emerald Crab has plenty of food, it is safe with corals and other invertebrates. These creatures are omnivorous and opportunistic; when hungry, they will turn their attention to fish, corals and other invertebrates. Luckily most reefs create a constant supply of food, so this is rarely a cause for concern. If your reef is too clean, supplement with meaty fish foods and algae sheets.

Emerald Crabs grow to two and a half inches long. They are territorial towards their own species, so keep only one Emerald Crab per 40 pounds of live rock.

Halloween Hermit Crab (Ciliopagurus strigatus)

Halloween Hermit Crab

The colorful Halloween Hermit Crab has brilliant red legs with bright orange bands. These crabs will eat hair algae, cyanobacteria, detritus and uneaten food. Halloween Hermits will also sift through sand looking for food.

Halloween Hermit Crabs grow large, about two inches long, and their shells can knock down loose corals and small rocks. They are relatively peaceful and safe with corals and other invertebrates. As the crab grows, keep various sized empty shells in aquarium; remember that it can pull snails out of their shells.

Red Tip Hermit Crab (Clibanarius sp.)

Red Tip Hermit Crabs

Red Tip Hermit Crabs also known as Red Leg Hermit Crabs are small, peaceful and very similar to Blue Leg Crabs. Growing to a scant inch long allows it to clean in tight places. It has a great appetite for nuisance algae, including green hair and cyanobacteria.

Red Tip Hermit Crabs are safe for corals and most other invertebrates; they may attack snails for their shells.

Red Tip Hermit crabs are omnivores. If food is scarce, feed these crabs Nori algae sheets.

Scarlet Reef Hermit Crab (Paguristes cadenati)

Scarlet Reef Hermit Crab

Scarlet Reef Hermit Crabs are very hardy and some of the best choices for a reef aquarium. Easy to recognize with its bright red legs and a red body, Scarlet Reef Hermit Crabs spend their lives searching and eating nuisance filamentous algae, red cyanobacteria and detritus.

The Scarlet Reef Hermit Crab will only grow to one and a half inches in length. This crab is safe with corals and most invertebrates. On occasional they are known to attack snails for their shells. They are peaceful with tank mates and their own kind.

They are omnivores and will eat excess fish foods and Nori seaweed or any food that is high in spirulina, kelp and other forms of algae.

Zebra Hermit Crab (Calcinus laevimanus)

Zebra Hermit Crab

A Zebra Hermit Crab is a great choice for a mini reef. It gets its name from the black and white bands on its legs and pinchers. Also known as the Left Handed Hermit Crab, this crab will withdraw into its shell for protection and use its large left claw to block the entrance.

Zebra Hermit Crabs are great scavengers with voracious appetites for filamentous algae like green hair algae, cyanobacteria (red slime algae) and detritus.

NOTE: They are one of the few true herbivore crabs.

If food is scarce, feed these crabs Nori algae sheets.

Although they are peaceful and reef safe, they will attack and kill snails for their shells.

Arrow Crab (Stenorhynchus seticornis)

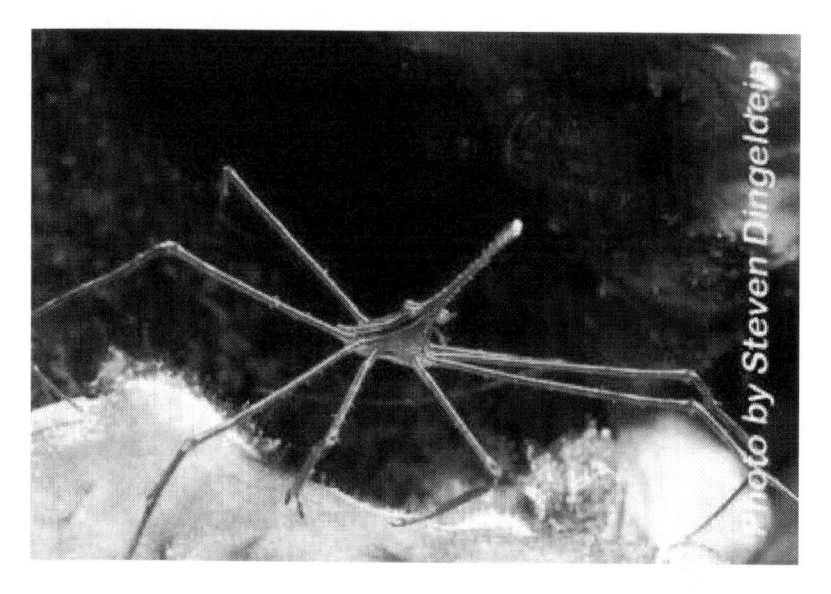

Arrow Crab

Photo by Steven Dingeldein

An Arrow Crab has long spindly legs with a narrow body and a long pointed head. It is also called a spider crab. This crab will crawl on rocks and sand in search of food. At feeding, an Arrow Crab will literally run across an aquarium to grab a chunk of food. It is territorial and will fight off fish and invertebrates to protect its food.

Arrow Crabs are very hardy and can grow to over six inches in length from leg to leg. Only keep one Arrow Crab in aquariums less than 55 gallons. They are beneficial carnivores, great scavengers of meaty food and will eat nuisance worms such as Bristleworms. They are a fun, unique crab to watch.

> *CAUTION: Add this crab to your reef only if you have a problem with bristleworms! Arrow Crabs may eat Xenia, feather dusters, coral polyps and attack other crabs and shrimp. It is nocturnal and can harm fish at night.*

Fan Worms

Feather Dusters look like a cluster of feathers sticking out of a tube. A worm creates this soft, flexible tube around its body for protection. The feathery part that sticks out of the tube is called the crown or fan, and at its base is the worm's mouth.

When a Feather Duster is frightened or concerned it will quickly pull its crown into its tube for protection. If highly stressed, it may even shed its crown; it will usually grow a new one.

In a reef aquarium, gently bury the Feather Duster's tube under the sand so that the crown is pointing upward into light current. At feeding time the Feather Duster will spread its crown to capture food floating in the water. Captured food is moved by cilia (hair-like motile projection) down a groove to the mouth. This filter feeder eats phytoplankton as well as fine detritus from the water. There are also many prepared liquid and frozen foods for filter feeders.

Reef aquariums stocked with numerous filter feeders may want to feed daily. If there are few filter feeders in the reef, feed them just a few times a week. A turkey baster may be used to lightly blow food into the current moving towards the crown. If you try to blow food directly at the crown it will retract into its tube.

Feather Dusters are hardy, easy to keep and peaceful with their tank mates. They are safe with corals and other invertebrates.

Hawaiian Feather Duster (Sabellastarte sp.)

Feather Dusters

Also called the Giant Feather Duster, Hawaiian Feather Dusters can grow up to seven inches long with a crown reaching seven inches in diameter. The crown can be tan with dark brown bands or tan or brown with white bands. These earthy colors do not make them sound exciting but they add a beauty and unique oddity to a reef.

Dwarf Feather Duster (Bispira sp.)

Dwarf Feather Duster

This animal can grow up to four inches long. The tube is a light brown color and the crown can be red and white, pink and white, lime green, white and yellow.

Coco Worm (Protula bispiralis)

Coco Worm and close up of a red and white crown

Coco Worms are unique among fan worms because they secrete a hard calcium carbonate protective tube around their bodies. Sticking out of the open end of the tube is a beautiful crown with feathery rays in shades of pink, yellow, red, orange or white or some combination of these colors.

Coco Worms create a hard, calcareous tube up to 24 inches long with interesting bends or spirals delineated along its length. When frightened or concerned this worm will quickly pull its filter feeding crown into its tube for protection.

Feather-shaped rays of the crown are used to collect food from water. Cilia move food particles down the ray to the mouth of the worm. Coco worms do not have a trap door (operculum) at the open end of the tube to keep the air out if lifted out of the water. When transporting this creature, fill a fish bag with aquarium water and place the coco worm in the bag taking care to keep it totally submersed.

Place the Coco Worm in a shaded place in the rockwork or on the sand. If placed on the sand, gently bury its tube under the sand so its crown is pointing upward, or place it in a hole or crevice in the rockwork where the crown receives light current.

These filter feeders eat phytoplankton, zooplankton, bacteria, and even fine detritus floating in the water. Supplement their natural diet with prepared liquid and frozen foods that contain phytoplankton and zooplankton. In a well-stocked reef with other filter feeders, you can feed daily; if you have a few filter feeders, feed them only a few times a week. A turkey baster may be used to lightly blow food into the current towards the crown. If you try to blow food directly at the crown it will retract into its tube and will not eat.

Like stony corals, the Coco Worm requires calcium carbonate to grow its calcareous tube, so be sure to add calcium and carbonate to a reef housing this creature.

Coco Worms are safe with all corals and invertebrates, but some crabs may pester the Coco Worm, causing it to retract. If a crab persistently bothers a Coco Worm such that its crown is retracted the majority of the time, it is time to remove the crab.

Sea Stars
Brittle Star and Serpent Star

Harlequin Serpent Star

There are up to 2000 species of starfish documented but few are considered reef-safe. The majority of Brittle Stars and Serpent Stars are considered reef safe.

Brittle Stars and Serpent Stars usually spend their days hiding in the rockwork or sand below it. This type of starfish will normally stay in the shelter of the rocks and reach its arms out to grab meaty foods drifting by, pulling the food back to its mouth. Brittle Stars and Serpent Stars are carnivores, making them excellent scavengers of detritus and uneaten fish food.

These starfish will burrow into the sand and move around helping to keep the sand substrate oxygenated.

Starfish in these family stay small and medium size and are safe with corals and other invertebrates. Larger stars such as a Green Brittle Star can capture and eat fish and motile invertebrates like hermit crabs.

Sand Sifting Sea Star (Astropecten polycanthus)

Sand Sifting Sea Star

Sand Sifting Sea Star makes a great addition to a reef's clean-up crew. They are peaceful and help keep the sand clean.

This star burrows into the sand in a most interesting manner (they appear to slowly vanish) in search of food, thus oxygenating the sand. When an aquarium is setup, the sand in the bottom of the aquarium is white or light tan. Over time, algae, detritus, bacteria, etc. grow on the sand making it dark and dingy. Servicing the reef by vacuuming the gravel while changing part of the water will help clean this up, but the sand will slowly start turning dark again. A Sand Sifting Sea Star 'churns' the sand, giving it a cleaner appearance.

Sand Sifting Sea Stars are omnivores. They eat detritus, small crustacean, microfauna (microscopic animals) and uneaten foods. They are most active at night after the lights go out. In a large, established reef there may be enough food for the starfish. In cleaner aquariums it is best to supplement their diet with a small amount of fish food such as mysis shrimp. Feed them at night when the fish are resting. One Sand Sifting Sea Star can usually keep the sand in a 90 gallon tank clean.

Sand Sifting Sea Star is peaceful and grow to around six inches in an aquarium and up to eight inches or larger in the ocean. This Sea Star is safe with corals, but like most starfish, they can eat small bivalves like clams and urchins and shrimp.

Shrimp

Shrimp, like crabs, periodically molt their external skeleton (exoskeleton) to grow. A shrimp may hide for several days while its new exoskeleton hardens. When they shed their exoskeleton it will look identical to the shrimp including the antennas, except it will be hollow. When you see it lying on the bottom of the aquarium and it is empty it means your shrimp now has a pretty new and slightly larger exoskeleton.

Blood Red Fire Shrimp (Lysmata debelius)

Blood Red Fire Shrimp

Fire Shrimp are very striking with their deep red body with white dots, long white antennae and white front legs. This cleaner shrimp uses its long white antennas to attract fish swimming by that want to be cleaned.

Fire Shrimp grow to about two inches long and spend most of their time hanging upside down in their favorites spot in a cave or under a ledge. They are more likely to remain hidden among the rock work than Scarlet Skunk Cleaner Shrimp which are usually out in the open. Fire shrimp can be kept individually, in pair or in a group. They also mix well with other shrimp.

At feeding time, Fire Shrimp will dart of their hiding place, run after and grab bits of meaty foods and retreat.

Like other cleaner shrimp, Fire Shrimp can set up a "cleaning station" in a mini reef. They actually pick parasites and dead tissue off their fishy tank mates. A fish will come to the cleaning station and hold its body close to the shrimp so it can climb on. Besides cleaning its body, this shrimp can also do dental work, cleaning inside the mouth of the fish.

Fire Shrimp are hardy once established in a reef. They are safe with corals and invertebrates.

Candy Stripe Pistol Shrimp (Alpheus randalli) and Tiger Snapping Shrimp (Alpheus bellulus)

Look closely the Candy Stripe Pistol Shrimp is at the bottom of Yasha White Ray Shrimp Goby

    The Pistol or Snapping Shrimp get their name by the cracking sound that their powerful, enlarged claw makes when it quickly closes. Candy Stripe Pistol Shrimp and Tiger Snapping Shrimp are two of the most commonly kept species.
    Candy Stripe Pistol Shrimp, as its name suggests, is a pretty shrimp with red and white alternating stripes. A Tiger Snapping Shrimp is drab in comparison with its tan body and dark bands. Candy Stripe Pistol Shrimp will grow to about 2 inches long while the Tiger Snapping Shrimp grows larger up to three inches.
    One of the most captivating characteristics about some Pistol Shrimp is their symbiotic relationship with Gobies. A Pistol Shrimp

and Goby will live together in a burrow which the shrimp excavated. The shrimp will maintain the burrow while the Goby stands guard near the entrance. When a predator comes near, the Goby alerts the Pistol Shrimp. They both hide in the burrow until the danger is gone. They will also sleep together in their burrow. A few Gobies that will pair up with Candy Stripe Pistol Shrimp and Tiger Snapping Shrimp are the Hi Fin Red Banded Goby, Yasha White Ray Shrimp Goby and Yellow Watchman Goby.

NOTE: Not all Pistol Shrimps will team up with a goby.

Make sure the sand is at least one and a half inches deep for these shrimp to make their burrow. When adding a Pistol Shrimp to a reef you do not know where he will build his burrow.

These shrimp are carnivorous scavengers eating any meaty food that comes near its burrow.

Pistol shrimp are safe with corals and most invertebrates, but can eat shrimp smaller than themselves.

Peppermint Shrimp (Lysmata wurdemanni)

Peppermint Shrimp

Peppermint Shrimp are small, easy to care for and can be beneficial in a mini reef. They are inexpensive compared to some of the more colorful shrimp.

Peppermint Shrimp are hardy and grow to two inches long. They can be red or a light pink with dark red stripes and bands on its body. Add one Peppermint Shrimp or add a group of them, they will get along together. They also live well with other peaceful shrimp.

Peppermint Shrimp generally hide in the rockwork during the day and run out at feeding time. They are most active during the night and you can watch their activities with moonlights (a few blue LED lights.) They will venture over the entire aquarium looking for food.

They are great eaters of meaty food and detritus. Given the chance they will steal food from corals and anemones. To feed corals it is a good practice to put food for the shrimp at the opposite end of the aquarium before attempting to target-feed corals.

The Peppermint Shrimp is highly sought after for its ability to eat nuisance aiptasia or glass anemones. They are several species sold under the trade name Peppermint Shrimp, but choose only shrimp collected from the Atlantic and gulf coast region if you want them to chow down on aiptasia.

Peppermint shrimp are generally reef safe, but they will occasionally aggravate corals by ripping food out of coral polyps.

Scarlet Skunk Cleaner Shrimp (Lysmata amboinensis)

Scarlet Skunk Cleaner Shrimp

The Scarlet Skunk Cleaner Shrimp is one of my personal favorites. It is easy to identify with two red stripes and one white stripe in the middle going down its back. It has long white antennas that are used to attract fish that need a cleaner shrimp.

Scarlet Skunk Cleaner Shrimp are peaceful, hardy and easy to keep. They only grow to two inches in length but when you see the adults they look much larger because of their long antennas. Keep one or several together in a reef. Unlike Fire Shrimp, Scarlet Skunk Cleaner Shrimp will stay out in the open. Both of these shrimp will live in the same aquarium but will stay in different spots among the rocks.

This Cleaner Shrimp can set up a "cleaning station" in a mini reef where they will pick parasites and dead tissue off fish tank mates. A fish will come to the cleaning station and hold its body close to the shrimp so it can climb on. The fish will stay in the cleaning station area while the shrimp cleans it body. Cleaner shrimp will remove and eat Ich, a common parasite that attaches to saltwater fish. It can also perform dental cleaning inside the mouth of the fish.

They are carnivores and greedily nab any meaty food that enters the aquarium. At feeding time it can swim into the water column and compete with peaceful fish for food.

Scarlet Skunk Cleaner Shrimp are safe with corals and invertebrates. The only downside is this shrimp may try to steal food from corals which you are target feeding (explained in Feeding Corals.) In this case, feed these shrimp well before feeding corals.

Snails

Astraea Snail (Astraea tecta)

Astraea Snail

The Astraea Snail has a unique pyramid-shaped spiral shell with grooves along the outer perimeter. These snails are peaceful, easy to keep and grow to about an inch long.

Astraeas are herbivores that consume film algae such as diatoms, short filamentous algae and cyanobacteria off the rock work. They will also clean algae off the walls of the aquarium.

While safe to mix with corals and other invertebrates, this snail cannot turn itself over in the sand. It needs either a rock or side of the aquarium to grip onto to upright itself. When introducing an Astraea Snail to an aquarium, make sure to turn the shell such that its opening is on the sand or rock. If you notice a snail is on its back, turn the shell. If left upside down they will eventually die or become food for other tank inhabitants such as a hermits crab.

Add one Astraea Snail for each 10 gallons of water; supplement feed with dried Nori seaweed or a food that is high in spirulina, kelp and other forms of algae.

Banded Trochus Snail (Trochus sp.)

Banded Trochus Snail

Banded Trochus Snails are some of the best snails for the reef. They are peaceful, easy to keep and have a distinctive pyramid-shaped shell.

This snail is an herbivore with a voracious appetite for film algae, cyanobacteria, and diatoms on live rock, sand, and sides of the aquarium.

Banded Trochus Snails grow to an inch high. Its pyramid shape shell makes it unlikely to knock down rocks or corals from the rockwork. They spend most of the day hiding and come out to eat in the dark.

One benefit to keeping Banded Trochus Snails in a reef aquarium is that they may actually breed and populate the reef. They can also turn themselves over if they happen to fall, unlike Astraea and Mexican Turbo Snails that simply lay there and die or get eaten by crabs.

Banded Trochus Snails are safe with corals and other invertebrates.

Cerith Snail (Cerithium sp.)

Cerith Snails

Cerith Snails are ideal for a reef aquarium given their diverse appetite. They have a small conical shaped shell and grow to a little over an inch long. They can fit into and clean tight places in rocks and within coral polyps.

These snails consume detritus, uneaten food, film algae, hair algae, cyanobacteria and diatoms in the sand, on the rocks and attached to the sides of the aquarium. Cerith Snails are nocturnal and may not be very active during the day. They are hardy, peaceful and you may find them buried in the sand.

Cerith Snails are safe with corals and other invertebrates. Their small size and varied tastes makes them a great addition to a cleaning crew. Add one per ten gallons of aquarium water.

Mexican Turbo Snail (Turbo fluctuosa)

Mexican Turbo Snail

The Mexican Turbo Snail is one of the larger snails and gets its name from its thick turban-shaped shell.

The Mexican Turbo Snail is peaceful, easy to keep and grows to over two inches. Mexican Turbo Snails are herbivores and voraciously eat nuisance micro algae, filamentous algae like green and red hair algae and diatoms off rockwork and sides of aquarium.

While searching for food their large shells can knock down loose rocks and corals.

A Mexican Turbo Snail is safe with corals and other invertebrates. This snail cannot turn itself over in the sand. It needs either a rock or side of the aquarium to grip and upright itself. When introducing a Mexican Turbo Snail into an aquarium, turn its shell such that the opening is on the sand. If left upside down this snail will eventually die and be eaten by other tank inhabitants such as a hermits crab.

Mexican Turbo Snails are good additions to the cleanup crew. Add one snail per every 20 to 40 gallons of water. Adding a few at a time ensures they have an ongoing food source. If the food becomes limited, feed them dried Nori seaweed or a food that is high in spirulina, kelp and other forms of algae.

Nassarius Snail (Nassarius sp.)

Nassarius Snail

Nassarius Snails are excellent for a reef aquarium because they help keep the sand clean, stirred and oxygenated.

The most exciting feature about Nassarius Snails takes place during feeding. Nassarius Snails spend most of their time under the sand, usually with their proboscis (long flexible tube) sticking above the sand to alert them when food is present. As soon as it senses food in the aquarium it quickly emerges from the sand. It is neat to watch numerous Nassarius Snails emerge from the sand at the same time, reminiscent of an old horror movie where the living dead rise from their graves.

Nassarius Snails from Tonga are some of the largest and hardiest snails available, growing up to an inch long. Nassarius Snails glide across the sand and glass at record snail speeds.

Nassarius Snails are carnivores and thrive on uneaten meaty foods, detritus and fish waste. They are safe with corals and other invertebrates. Nassarius Snails should be part of the cleanup crew.

Nerite Snail (Nerita sp.)

Nerite Snail

A Nerite Snail is a great small scavenger with a rounded shell. The Caribbean variety has a pretty black and white wavy zebra-like pattern on its shell.

Nerite Snails are herbivores that eat detritus, film and hair algae, diatoms and cyanobacteria. These snails do a great job of cleaning the rock work and walls of an aquarium.

The Nerite Snail is peaceful, easy to keep and grow to about an inch long. Their small size and smooth shells generally keep them for knocking down loose rocks or corals. Nerite Snails tend to be active at night.

Nerite Snails are voracious algae eaters and, if needed, their diet can be supplemented with Nori seaweed or a food that is high in spirulina, kelp and other forms of algae.

Nerite Snails are safe with corals and invertebrates. Add one snail for each 10 gallons of aquarium water.

Tridacna Clams

Tridacna Maxima - three of the many colors and patterns

Some varieties of Tridacna Clams are the most stunning purple, blue and green colors you will find in the ocean. When a clam opens up it has a thin membrane or mantle surrounding the body of the clam. It is in this mantle that exhibits those amazing colors.

Tridacna Clams can do well in an established aquarium and are not for the beginner. Keeping these clams thriving will entail time researching a specific species before making a purchase. Here are some highlights about Tridacna Clams.

Tridacna Clams, like corals, house symbiotic algae called zooxanthellae. This algae provides most of the food and nutrients the clams needs. Tridacna Clams are also filter feeders and can help maintain good water quality by absorbing nitrates and other organics

Tridacna Derasa is easiest to keep and hardiest of the Tridacna clams. It can grow up to 24 inches across in the wild. Tridacna Derasas are slow growers, they live on the sand, and are more tolerant of lower light then other clams but should be placed away from rockwork and corals so as not to shade it.

Tridacna Crocea are unique in the fact that they bore into the rock and attach themselves with a byssal or filament. They are very disease resistant and require intense light.

Tridacna Maxima clams need intense light and should generally be placed on a rock close to the light. This clam does best in bright light like that which Metal Halides produce. Tridacna Maxima will attach itself to rocks with its byssal. In the wild they can grow up to a foot long.

Tridacna Squamosa, like the Tridacna Derasa, prefer to live on the sand. If placed on rocks the Squamosa will move itself from the rocks and fall to the sand.

Care should be taken anytime you move a clam so you do not damage its byssal. Sand dwelling claims will usually anchor themselves to the aquarium bottom, making them difficult to move. If you ever need to move a clam, place a small flat rock under the sand and place the clam on it. Now the clam will attached its byssal to the rock and can be moved without damage or stress.

Sea Urchins

Sea Urchins are unique and interesting but not recommended for most reef aquariums. They have a spherical or oval shape shell covered with spines for protection. Sea Urchins are found in a variety of colors including purple, red, brown, black and light pink.

Most sea urchins are great at eating many types of algae including coralline algae. Coralline algae will grow on rocks, encrusting them in a pleasant pink or purple color. It is beneficial since its hard calcium structure keeps some algae from taking hold and growing on live rock. If you like the way coralline algae looks, then limit the number of urchins you keep.

If you have a bad nuisance algae problem you can add several Urchins since they are relatively easy to catch and remove once algae is under control.

Sea Urchins usually stay in one place during the day and are active at night. They are bulldozers that can knock down substantial size rocks and corals as they munch along.

Another downside to keeping Urchins is they can eat and damage certain corals. Several species of urchins will try to protect themselves from predators by sticking pieces of algae, shells, pebbles, loose frags (small corals), zooanthid colonies onto their spines. Some Urchins will eat coral polyps.

You do not need an urchin to create a well balanced reef. It is safer to use crabs and snails to control algae. If you still choose to add a sea urchin, the Blue Tuxedo Urchin (Mespilia globulus) is one of the best choices.

Blue Tuxedo Urchin (Mespilia globulus)

Blue Tuxedo Urchin

Blue Tuxedo Urchin has short spines and blue bands without spines. It does a great job eating algae and may eat beneficial coralline algae. They are easy to keep and grow up to three inches long.

Like other urchins, the Blue Tuxedo is up at night foraging for algae and uneaten food on rocks, sand and sides of aquarium and rest during the day. They have very sharp spines so take care when handling or transporting them. If you keep zooanthid colonies in your reef, Blue Tuxedo Urchin may pull them loose and carry them around as camouflage along with, algae, shells etc.

Anemone

Bubble Tip and Long Tentacle Anemones

Anemones are well known for their symbiotic relationship with clownfish. Most of us have seen pictures of Clownfish hiding or playing in the tentacles of a sea anemone.

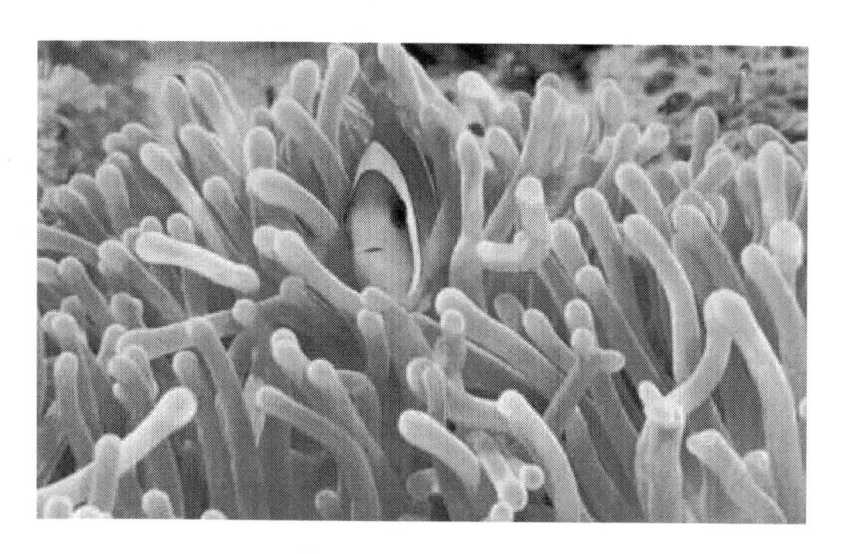

Clownfish relaxing in its Anemone

Clownfish will hide in an anemone for protection and share food with the anemone. While an anemone will live well in a reef aquarium with or without a Clownfish, they may not be an ideal choice for a reef aquarium.

Anemones have either a tubular or flat-shaped body with tentacles that are coated with stinging cells (nematocysts) used to paralyze small swimming animals. These tentacles are also used to push food towards its mouth.

Anemones attach themselves to rocks, sides of the aquarium or anywhere else they desire. You can try to place an anemone in a certain place in a reef and he may stay there, but there is a better chance that he will choose another spot. Sometimes an anemone will choose a great spot where it is visible; other times it will attach itself totally out of view behind the rockwork. They can also choose a spot beside your prize coral... stinging it to death.

Often, while the anemone slithers along looking for its perfect location, it will sting and damage corals along the way. It is not easy to move an anemone once it attaches to a rock. Many times you end up tearing its flesh to get it free. For these reasons, it is preferable to keep anemones without corals.

Anemones are like coral in that they both have symbiotic algae (zooxanthellae) living in their tissue which, through photosynthesis, creates nutrients (carbohydrates) for the anemone. They can also be fed meaty foods such as brine shrimp, squid, krill pieces or chopped fish.

When anemones feel threatened or need to expel waste they will deflate their tentacles and bodies. Reef tanks provide ideal conditions for anemones where they can grow to be quite large. As mentioned, though, there is that downside as they sting corals to death. If you choose to add an anemone, dutifully watch the corals around it.

A few popular anemones are the Rose Bulb Anemone (Entacmaea quadricolor), Long Tentacle Anemone (Macrodactyla doreensis) and Sebae Anemone (Heteractis crispa.)

Bringing Your New Invertebrates Home

Acclimation Method

1. Turn off the aquarium light to avoid stressing the invertebrates.

2. Float the sealed bag with the invertebrates inside the aquarium or sump water for 15 to 30 minutes. The salesperson should have filled at least half the bag with air, enabling the bag to float in your aquarium. Floating the bag allows the water in the bag to gradually change to the same temperature as the aquarium water.

3. Put a clean, nontoxic or food-grade container or bucket in front of the aquarium. The number and size of the invertebrates you are adding to your aquarium determines the size of the bucket you will need. For twelve small snails, for example, a one gallon container will do.

NOTE: When acclimating new invertebrates make sure you keep it in a separate container from fish and corals that you acclimate at the same time.

4. Once the temperature of the water in the plastic bag is the same as the water in the aquarium, open the bag and pour the inverts gently into the bucket. If there is not enough water to cover the invertebrates,

place something under one side of the bucket to make a pocket of deep water inside.

Invertebrates released into bucket of water

NOTE: This slow acclimation method will slowly raise the ph as well as level out other water parameters including specific gravity.

5. Add an ammonia neutralizing product to the bucket of water with the invertebrates. There are several products available at aquarium stores which will quickly neutralize ammonia.

6. Start a siphon to slowly drip water from your aquarium into the container. The siphon is a section of airline tubing generally four to six feet long with an adjustable valve on one end.

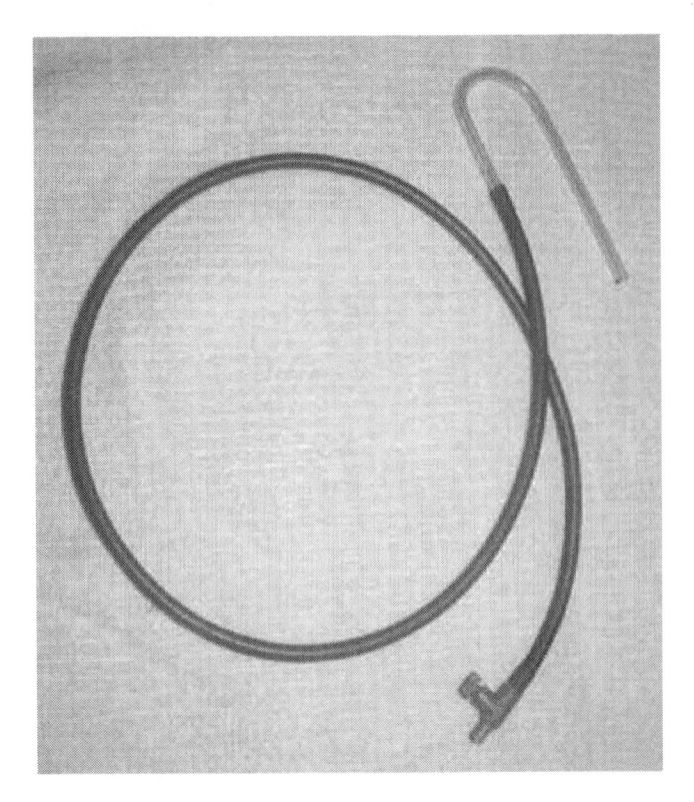

Drip line with plastic u-shape pipe to hang on rim of aquarium, airline tubing and valve

Place the end of the tubing without the valve in your aquarium or sump if it is high enough off the ground to create a flow; then suck on the valve end to begin water flow. Place the tubing in the bucket and slowly open and close the valve until it drips two to four drops per second.

Water from aquarium slowly dripping into bucket

7. Cover the bucket to keep invertebrates like snails from climbing out and to keep the drip bucket dark.

8. When the water in the bucket has doubled, dip out about half of the water and discard.

9. Let the water level double again.

10. Test the pH of the water in the bucket. If it matches the water of the aquarium acclimation is complete. If not continue the drip method until pH of the bucket matches your reef.

11. Next, transfer the invertebrates to the aquarium using a fish net or small plastic container. **Make sure all snails are turned so the shell opening is against the sand or rock.**

NOTE: DO NOT add water from the fish bag to your aquarium as this water will most likely have different parameters than your aquarium. Fish stores may have also added medication to their water, so it is sensible to simply throw that water away.

12. Add premixed saltwater to the aquarium to replace water just removed for acclimation.

Follow these tips as well:

TIPS:

Feed a small amount of food to help distract the original tank inhabitants from picking on the new invertebrates.

Leave the aquarium light off for a few hours to give invertebrates a chance to acclimate

When new invertebrates enter the aquarium it is normal behavior to see territorial disputes.

Chapter 7

Selecting and Placing Corals

Live corals can transform an ordinary saltwater fish aquarium into a beautiful, vibrant underwater world. Corals are available in nearly every color imaginable and in a huge variety of shapes and sizes. Some sway with water currents while others tower majestically in brilliant blues, purples, reds and greens.

To help simplify the many different types of corals, we will separate them into three groups: Soft Corals, Long Polyp Stony (LPS) Corals and Short Polyp Stony (SPS) Corals. These divisions allow for a simple understanding of coral care and compatibility.

Soft Coral General Information

Soft Corals are available in many beautiful shapes and colors. Most have soft flexible bodies allowing them to move and sway with water currents. Soft Corals lack a true skeleton and are made up of numerous polyps connected by tissue. A polyp is an invertebrate which has a mouth, stomach, tentacles and reproductive organs. Since they do not have a skeleton they can inflate by taking on seawater or deflate by expelling seawater. Soft Corals can also extend and withdraw their tentacles.

Living within the cell walls of most coral polyps is a symbiotic algae, zooxanthellae, which create nutrients through photosynthesis. While photosynthetic corals obtain most essential nutrients from zooxanthellae, many will benefit from eating small to microscopic phytoplankton, zooplankton, brine shrimp and commercial filter feeder foods.

The majority of photosynthetic Soft Corals are easy to keep and great for beginning reef keepers. Most Soft Corals require low to medium light and can tolerate less than ideal water conditions. Nearly all are fast growers and easy to propagate.

For the most part, Soft Corals need medium to strong water movement created by water pumps, power heads and wave makers. Water flow should be alternating from several directions intermittently. This variable or alternating water current helps to remove detritus which settles on corals as well as waste created by the coral itself. Corals also rely on this water flow to bring them food.

Some Soft Corals use calcium carbonate from the surrounding water to produce tiny spicules or sclerites in their tissue giving them texture and support. Other Soft Corals will use calcium carbonate to form an attachment to the substrate.

Soft Corals and hard corals have tentacles with stinging cells called nematocysts that they use to paralyze food. These tentacles can also be used to sting corals placed close by. Many Soft Corals also have a chemical defense; they release the chemical into the water to damage or obstruct the growth of nearby corals. The level of toxicity varies by genus. To reduce the toxin, use a high grade activated filter carbon in the filter. Always leave space between corals to compensate for aggression and growth.

Information on keeping individual species or groups of Soft Corals is provided later, separated into section on Mushrooms, Leathers, Zoanthids, Star Polyps, Xenias and more.

LPS and SPS General Information

Long Polyp Stony (LPS) Corals and Short Polyp Stony (SPS) Corals have a hard skeleton and are often referred to as stony corals. They can be made up of a single polyp or multiple polyps called colonies. Living in the cell walls of many stony coral polyps is the symbiotic algae zooxanthellae, which through photosynthesis produces nutrients. These polyps use nutrients for energy. They take calcium carbonate from saltwater so that they can secrete a hard, cup-shaped skeleton to protect the polyp.

Most stony corals are made up of hundreds or thousands of these little polyps, forming a coral colony. Generations upon generation of polyps are the building blocks of huge coral reefs. Polyps live on the surface of these hard corals.

LPS Coral has the larger size polyps and are easier to keep then SPS Corals. They are hardy and do not require as intense light as SPS, or as much water movement. Water movement in an aquarium is created by water pumps, power heads and wave makers. Water flow should be alternating from several directions, with intermittent flow. This variable or alternating current helps to remove detritus which settles on corals. Corals also rely on water flow to bring them food. SPS Corals need medium to high, variable and turbulent water flow.

To determine the correct flow of water, make certain that the polyps sway, expand and contract. Too much or too little water flow can cause polyps to retract. Adjust your flow such that polyps fully extend.

NOTE: If the water flow is ideal and the polyps still stay closed this can indicate too much light. Polyps contract to protect themselves and zooxanthellae from excessive light.

Numerous stony corals have stinging cells in specialized tentacles called sweeper tentacles. Depending on the toxicity of the stinging cells, they can kill or severely damage a competing coral. Competition derives from coral in close proximity to each other with one or more wanting more room, additional light, food, etc. These corals can extend sweeper tentacles in all directions or just at a competing coral. The lengths of these tentacles vary among coral species as do toxicity of stinging cells. As a general rule, leave at least six inches around an LPS Coral in all directions from other corals and sessile invertebrates. SPS Corals can be placed closer to each other with about two to three inches space in all directions.

Photosynthetic stony corals get most of their nutrients from their zooxanthellae and, depending on the coral species, also benefit from eating mysis shrimp, krill, minced raw seafood, zooplankton, phytoplankton and filter feeder foods. In the wild, coral polyps are nocturnal; they remain inside their skeletons during the day and extend their tentacles to feed at night. Once settled into an aquarium, most stony corals will extend feeding polyps during the day when they sense food in the water.

Genus Tubastraea, Sun Corals, do not house photosynthetic algae and must obtain all food from surrounding water. Non-photosynthetic corals MUST be fed regularly to survive.

Conclusion

The easiest corals to start a reef are either Soft Corals or LPS Corals. The Majority of SPS corals demand higher water quality, intense light and good water flow and are best left for experienced hobbyists.

Soft Corals

Kenya Tree Coral (Capnella sp.)

Kenya Tree Coral

Kenya Tree Corals are excellent beginner corals, resembling a tree with a thick trunk and lots of branches. Kenya Trees display groups of extended polyps on top of their branches.

This coral grows fairly fast to a height of around a foot. They are usually earthy in colors of light tan to brown but can also be found in a very attractive green.

They prefer moderate to high turbulent water current with medium to bright light and can thrive at almost any level in the reef with sufficient light.

Kenya Tree Corals do have zooxanthellae in their tissue but relies on their intake of phytoplankton and other prepared coral foods.

They are easy to propagate or frag; cut off a branch with a razor blade or sharp scissors and attach the cutting to a rock or reef plug with a rubber band or gel cyanoacrylate glue (Super Glue gel.) After a few days the cutting will attach itself to the rock. It can also produce frags itself by dropping off branches which will grow into new colonies.

Leather Corals

Leather Corals (family Alcyoniidae) are soft corals. We will focus on genus Alcyonium, Cladiella, Lobophytum, Sarcophyton and Sinularia as these include corals that are excellent for beginners.

Most Leather Corals are very hardy, relatively peaceful and have a leathery appearance. They are flexible and soft. Many Leather Corals grow quickly and rather large.

The majority of Leather Corals will retract their polyps, shrink and periodically form a mucus layer. This layer is shed or sloughed off to remove waste, algae and debris which have accumulated on the coral's surface. Medium to strong turbulent water flow can help with slime removal. Mucus and detritus can also be gently siphoned off with a turkey baster.

Most Leather Corals house zooxanthellae and require medium to high light. They do not require metal halide lighting to thrive. The majority of necessary nutrients are acquired through the zooxanthellae in their polyps' tissue, most will also eat small foods like zooplankton, phytoplankton and prepared filter feeder foods.

Leather Corals are also easy to propagate by cutting sections at least three inches long by one inch wide using a new razorblade. Attach the cuttings to a piece of rock or coral plug and place the cut end towards a current. The cutting will begin a new coral colony.

Colt Coral (Klyxum sp.)

Colt Coral

Colt Coral is a popular beginner coral for its ease of care, hardiness and attractiveness. It has a creamy to light colored stalk and branches with finger-like projections which have brown or greenish brown polyps. When the polyps extend it gives the coral a fluffy appearance.

Colt Corals can grow relatively quickly, up to 16 inches high, and often shade surrounding corals. They need moderate to strong turbulent water flow to help remove the large amounts of mucus they produce. Current directly hitting this coral may cause its polyps to stay closed.

Although they have symbiotic zooxanthellae algae in their tissue to produce most of their nutrients, they benefit from additional foods like micro-plankton, brine shrimp, and filter feeding foods.

Devil's Hand Leather Coral (Lobophytum sp.)

Devil's Hand Leather Coral

Devil's Hand Leather Coral is another great beginner coral with its thick, compact base and finger-like projections. Polyps are scattered throughout the fingers.

Devil's Hand Leather Coral, through aquaculture, is available in bright green, pink, blue, yellow, shades of brown and more. They produce less mucus and are more forgiving than other Leather Corals.

They can be placed at any level in the aquarium with adequate space around them and direct light.

Toadstool Mushroom Leather Coral (Sarcophyton sp.)

Toadstool Mushroom Leather Coral

Toadstool Mushroom Leather Coral is another easy coral that, as its name states, is shaped like a mushroom. It has a smooth stalk with a cap covered in numerous short polyps. It is very tranquil to watch the polyps sway with the current.

Toadstool Mushroom Leather Coral is available in tan, yellow, brown or green, with gold, green or white polyps. They can be placed at any level in the aquarium with adequate space around them as long as the area is not shaded by other coral or rockwork.

Cabbage Leather Coral (Sinularia brassica)

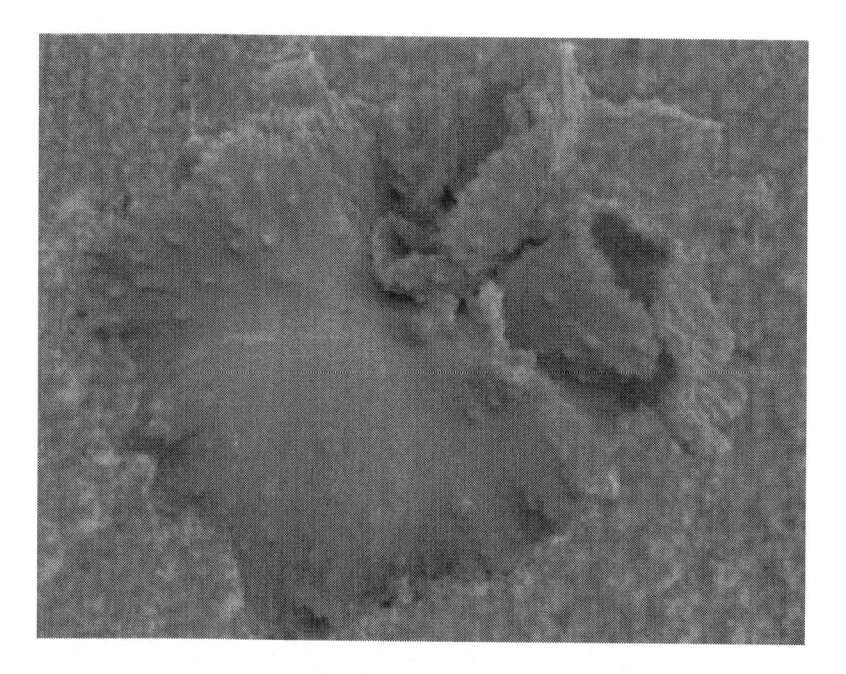

Cabbage Leather Coral

Cabbage Leather Coral is an eye-catching colony coral with small lobes shaped like cabbage leaves. These wide, relatively thick, and tough lobes grow on sturdy stalks. Cabbage Leathers can be yellow, green, purple, brown, tan, cream, pink, or gray.

This coral grows best in medium to bright light combined with moderate to strong water current. Give it ample room as it can grow quite large and may shade surrounding corals. It is generally peaceful although it can release toxins so space it away from other corals.

Cabbage Leather Coral are easy to keep, great for beginners and will readily reproduce on its own. Symbiotic algae, zooxanthellae, housed in its tissue provide most necessary nutrients. This coral will also benefit from additional foods like micro-plankton, brine shrimp, and filter feeding foods.

Finger Leather Coral (Sinularia sp.)

Finger Leather Corals

Finger Leather Corals are attractive, easy-to-keep and are great for beginners. This fast growing coral can reach over three feet in height, so give it plenty of room to grow. The most common color is tan or brown but they are also available in green, white, yellow, and gray.

Finger Leather Coral likes bright light, but because of its size it is best to place it in bottom half of the aquarium.

Mushroom

Green and blue Mushrooms

Mushrooms, from the genera Discosoma and Actinodiscus, are beautiful and available in many intense colors including red, blue, green and purple. They can also have striking patterns such as bull's-eye, striped, molted, spotted and more.

The mushrooms in these two genera are some of the best beginner corals. A Mushroom Coral has a short stem (usually not visible) with flattened disc that can be smooth, bumpy, or have a fuzzy appearance. They are readily available in most aquarium stores and are some of the easiest corals to keep.

Mushrooms can be as small as an inch; some varieties such as Elephant Ear Mushroom (Rhodactis mussoides) will grow to almost a foot in diameter. Most Mushrooms grow to around three inches in diameter and are very tolerant of fluctuating water quality.

Mushrooms prefer low to medium light. When kept in intense light, place them close to the bottom of the aquarium. They need slow to medium water flow and will usually multiply until they cover an entire rock. Mushrooms can also release their grip and drift in the water current to another area in an aquarium to start a new colony.

Mushrooms get most of their nutrients from zooxanthellae, however they can also eat dissolved and particulate matter as well as some zooplankton and prepared filter feeder foods.

Mushrooms have nematocysts or stinging cells and when they come into contact with SPS corals they can cause recession, so give them some space. They can also reproduce rather rapidly.

Polyps

Clove Polyp (Clavularia sp.)

Clove Polyps

Clove Polyps are not only easy to keep; they are fun to watch as they wave in the water current. Some look like groups of flowers while others resemble small palm trees.

They have eight fan-like tentacles at the top of each stalk. The polyps grow from a base encrusting over the rocks and sand. The tentacles are usually white, green, brown, tan, pink or purple with the centers of each tentacle usually an entirely different distinct color. Polyps grow to around two inches high.

Clove Polyps require medium lighting and can be placed at almost any level depending on intensity of the light in the reef. They need good water flow to supply them with necessary nutrients and to wash away detritus. They are not aggressive; however they can be stung by aggressive corals. Space them several inches away from other corals to allow the colony to grow.

The variety in which tentacles look like palm fronds are called Clavularia Viridisy and are an awesome sight to behold.

Clove Polyps receive the majority of their nutrition from the zooxanthellae within the polyps' tissue. They can also be fed commercial filter feeding foods.

Pulsing Xenia (Xenia sp.)

Pulsing Xenia

A colony of Pulsing Xenia is mesmerizing to watch with its feather-like polyps opening and closing quickly as they sway gently in the current.

Pulsing Xenia have thick, smooth stalks up to three inches long. Extending from the top of the stalk is a crown of feather-like polyps, each carried on a one to two inch stem. Pulsing Xenia can be white, off white, many shades of light brown and even a very light green. They prefer a moderate fluctuating water flow. Directing strong current at the colony may cause polyps to retract and remain closed.

When Pulsing Xenia is happy they are very fast-growing and will form a large colony. Many hobbyists will trade in some of their ever-increasing supply of Xenia at their local fish stores.

Some Xenia Corals may release chemicals that are thought to cause damage to stony corals, so use caution putting these two types of coral together.

Pulsing Xenia need moderate to bright light since all or almost all of their nutrients come from photosynthesis in their zooxanthellae. You may find your colony in a different spot than you originally placed it; Pulsing Xenia can move towards bright light to find a spot they like. It appears to thrive best in reefs with higher dissolved nutrients, so it is not ideal for a hobbyist who prefers a pristine reef.

Green Star Polyps (Pachyclavularia violacea/ Briareum sp)

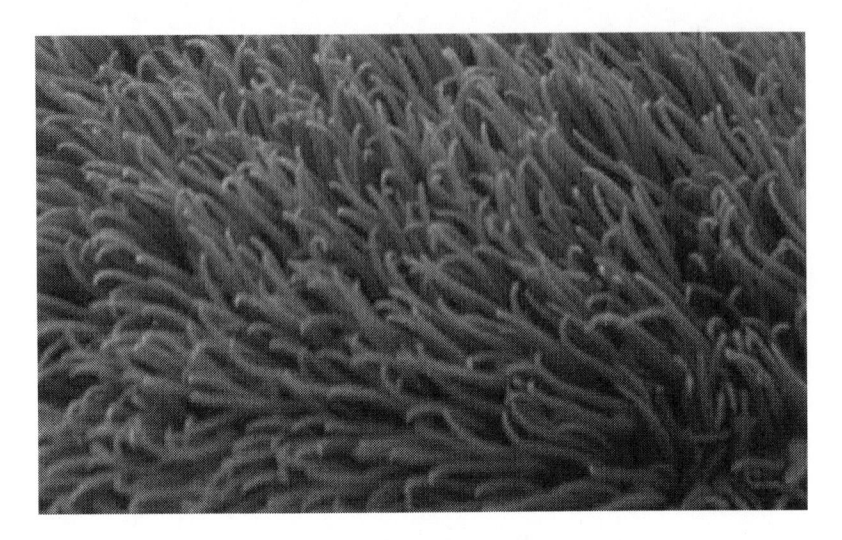

Green Star Polyps

Green Star Polyps are a gorgeous stunning mass of waving (via water current) short bright-green polyps. These polyps are half an inch long and connected together by a bright purple to reddish color base or mat. The polyps have eight smooth thin tentacles, which surround a center opening or mouth.

These polyps are easy to keep and can spread quickly, encrusting rocks, acrylic, and even glass. They are great for a beginner and their beautiful green waving movement adds dimension to a reef. They will not harm corals if they grow too close, but most corals will keep them at bay with their own protection.

Green Star Polyps need moderate to strong turbulent water flow and do best under medium to high light level. They receive the majority of their nutrition from the zooxanthellae within the polyps' tissue. Green Star Polyps can also be fed commercial filter feeding foods.

Place Green Start Polyps in the upper half of the aquarium. They are easy to propagate by cutting a section of the purple mat from the main colony using scissors or a razor blade. The cut piece (or frag) can be attached to a piece of rock with coral glue or gel cyanoacrylate glue (Super Glue gel.) A rubber band can also be used to hold the frag in place until the glue sets; it can be removed after a few days

Zoanthids
In the family Zoanthids we will focus on Zoanthus.

Zoanthus

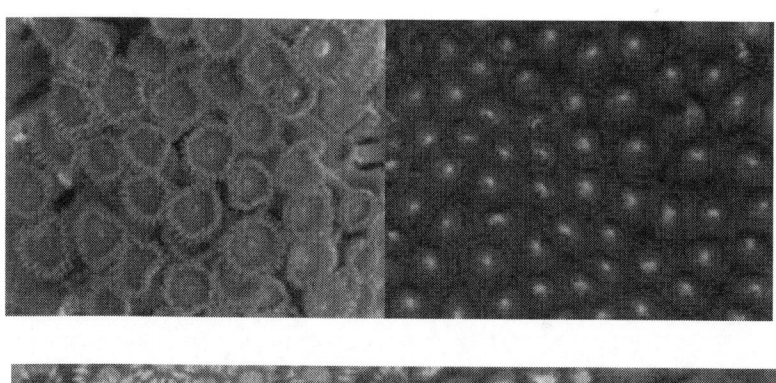

Multicolored Zoanthus

Zoanthus are easy to keep, great for a beginner and come in some spectacular colors. They are in high demand by hobbyists for their eye-catching colors and carpeting effect.

The majority of Zoanthus grow to about a half an inch high and are topped with a flat oral disc. Small tentacles extend from the outside of this disc. Zoanthus appear to form their colony with their polyps growing out of an encrusting mat or a fleshy tissue attached to the rockwork.

Different color Zoanthus colonies can be placed close to each other and over time will grow together creating beautiful carpeting with a patchwork of color. Just imagine how beautiful an aquarium looks like with a large colony of your favorite color Zoanthus.

The Genus Zoanthus are commonly called Zoas but are also often referred to by their family name Zoanthids. There are so many interesting color variations that it is difficult to identify Zoas, so hobbyists have created imaginative names to identify their amazing colorful designs and patterns. Names such as Bam Bam Orange, Fruit Loops, Kryptonite, Miami Vice, Papa Smurfs, Spiderman, Tropical Skittles and Tickle Me Pink are very descriptive.

Place Zoanthus in the top half of the aquarium as they require moderate to strong light to thrive. They also need medium flowing turbulent water. Under ideal conditions, Zoanthus can multiply quickly growing onto surrounding rocks and around corals. They have a mild sting which does not affect most corals. Zoanthus, if stung by anemones and aggressive corals, can die. The spreading colony mats can be trimmed and moved to other locations or even to another aquarium.

Zoanthus polyps contain the symbiotic algae zooxanthellae. With strong lighting and good water flow, Zoanthus will gain all the nutrients it needs to survive. If lighting is low, feed them a microplankton or prepared filter feeder food.

Zoanthus produce a weak toxin which can enter our bodies through a cut in our skin. To be on the safe side, wear gloves when handling them. Other species of Zoanthids like Palythoa produce a much stronger toxin.

Large Polyp Stony (LPS) Corals

Some hardy LPS stony corals are great for beginners as well as expert hobbyists.

Acanthastrea Lordhowensis Coral (Acanthastrea lordhowensis)

Acanthastrea Lordhowensis Coral - a sample of its many colors

Acanthastrea Lordhowensis Coral is highly sought after by novice and experienced hobbyist for their vibrant color combinations, hardiness and ease to keep. Their plump, meaty polyps cover their skeleton and come in numerous color combinations including blue, red, purple, orange, green, brown and ton more.

Acanthastrea Lordhowensis Coral is commonly called Acan Lord Coral. They prefer slow to medium turbulent water flow for filter feeding opportunities and to remove waste products from the coral.

Acan Lord Coral is able to adapt to all types of light intensity and seem to do well with moderate light. When using high intensity lighting, start Acan Lord Coral low in the aquarium and every few weeks move it up until it is at the desired location. They have long sweeper tentacles and can extend mesenterial filament bundles from their stomach, therefore give them at least six inches of space from the next coral or sessile invertebrate (i.e. Coco Worm.)

Acan Lord Coral gets most of their nutrients as they host zooxanthellae in their tissue but regular feeding will result in faster growth. These corals have feeding tentacles that are usually extended after the aquarium lights go out. These tentacles capture food floating by. They can also be target fed a few times a week with meaty seafood such as mysis shrimp, minced raw seafood and will also eat commercially prepared filter feeder foods.

Brain Coral, Lobophyllia (Lobophyllia hemprichii)

Lobophyllias sp.

Lobophyllia hemprichii Brain Coral has large fleshy meaty polyps which look like lobes or rounded projections which cover its skeleton. The polyps usually have a bumpy look and come in some beautiful colors including orange, bright red, green, steel blue and also some earthy tones.

This coral is easy to care for, requires medium water flow combined with medium to high intensity lights. Wild-caught specimens are collected from varying depths and therefore require different light intensities. To be safe, start your coral low in the aquarium and work it up towards the lights over a few weeks.

Lobophyllia Brain Coral have sweeper tentacles which are extended at night so give around six inches of space between it and adjacent corals. In addition, it has feeding tentacles which also normally come out after the lights are off. Feed this coral mysis shrimp, minced pieces of fish, Cyclops, plankton or a good filter feeder food once a week when tentacles are out. Most of their nutrients are gained from the symbiotic algae zooxanthellae that they host.

Brain Coral, Trachyphyllia (Trachyphyllia geoffroyi)

Trachyphyllia geoffroyi can be different colors; notice the distinct figure-eight shape

Trachyphyllia geoffroyi has a large fleshy polyp with its skeleton shaped in a figure eight configuration, or folded. This coral can be found in many bright color variations of green, red, pink, blue, as well as brown, and tan. Often called open Brain Coral, it needs medium to strong intensify light with moderate water current to help remove debris from their folds.

Trachyphyllia geoffroyi is found on the shallow ocean floor and does well in the sand in the bottom of an aquarium. Keep it away from sharp rocks so as not to tear the soft polyp.

With moderate light this coral does not have to be fed, but it can be fed once or twice a week at night or when the tentacles are extended. They will eat mysis, cyclops as well as minced meaty seafood.

Bubble Coral (Plerogyra sinuosa)

Bubble Corals

Bubble Coral is unique with its bubble-shaped polyps which look a tight bunch of grapes. The bubbles are typically a half to one inch in size and normally green, semi-transparent cream, or white.

This coral needs a low to medium turbulent water current strong enough to gently move the bubbles but not too much flow or it can keep them from completely expanding. The bubbles are filled with water during the day and at night they deflate revealing feeder tentacles and a sharp hard skeleton.

Bubble Coral prefer low to medium light and can be placed on the sand in the bottom of your aquarium. When placing this coral be sure there are no sharp rocks protruding into its space that could puncture its bubble-shaped tentacles as it fully inflates.

While Bubble Coral houses zooxanthellae in their polyps' tissue and gains some nutrients in this way, they should also be fed at least once a week meaty foods such as mysis shrimp, brine shrimp, chopped raw fish, and filter feeder foods. A turkey baster can be used to feed them directly.

They have long sweeper tentacles which can harm other corals. Space it about six inches away from other corals. Sweeper tentacles are usually out at night but occasionally you may see them during the day.

Cat's Eye Coral (Cynarina lacrymalis)

Red and Green Cat's Eye Coral

Cat's Eye Coral has a large fleshy center with a single, bubble-like polyp in a circular or oval surrounding it. Their translucent polyp can extend over twice the size of the skeleton. They are found in a variety of colors including bright pink, green and red as well as light and earthy tones. The center of the polyp can match the coral's color or may be an entirely different distinct color.

Cat's Eye Coral need low to medium intensity light along with low water movement to allow the polyp to fully open. Place this coral in the lower half of the aquarium, away from the rockwork. When it expands, sharp rocks can tear through its polyp. This is not an aggressive coral but it should still be spaced away from other corals.

At night the Cat's Eye Coral deflates and puts out long feeder tentacles. Even though it has zooxanthellae in its tissue to produce most of its nutrients, it can still benefit from feeding. Use minced raw fish, rock shrimp, mysis shrimp or other meaty seafood.

Doughnut Coral, Scolymia (Scolymia vitiensis)

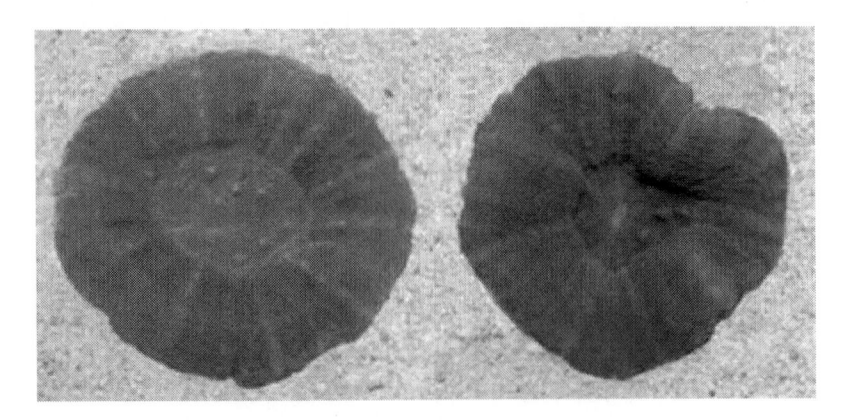

Green and red mixed Scolymia

Doughnut Coral as it names suggests is generally a round or dome-shaped, single, fleshy polyp with a depression in the center. Some have a flattened look and is therefore often referred to as Flat Brain Coral.

It looks similar to Cynarina but without the translucent bubble-shaped polyp. Doughnut Coral comes in beautiful bright green, red, and blue as well as some rather drab colors. They are often found in mottled or mixed colors.

Doughnut Coral prefer low to moderate water current. Strong currents may keep its polyps from fully expanding. These corals do well with moderately intense light. If your reef has intense light, it is best to place these corals on or near the bottom of the aquarium. With low to moderate light, place the coral in the upper half of the aquarium. This coral is not very aggressive but keep it a safe distance away from more aggressive corals.

Doughnut Corals grow fairly slow and get most of their nutrients from zooxanthellae. They extend feeding tentacles at night and can be target fed minced raw seafood, mysis shrimp and coral foods. Only feed when tentacles are extended.

This hardy, very easy to care for coral is great for beginners.

Candy Cane Coral (Caulastrea furcata)

Candy Cane Coral

Candy Cane Coral is another good beginner's coral. It is a single large fleshy round or oval polyp up to four inches in diameter on a stalk. These individual polyps form a branching colony with a beautiful cluster of polyps.

Candy Cane Coral are bright green, green, brown, burgundy, blue or yellow. They prefer low to moderate light and should be placed in the lower half of intensely lit aquariums. They require a medium flow of water current. Water flow may need to be reduced or turned off while feeding.

Candy Cane Coral have two-inch long sweeper tentacles which usually come out at night. These sweepers can inflict some damage to other corals, so leave plenty of space between corals.

Like most coral, Candy Cane Coral houses zooxanthellae and receives nutrients in that way, but it is also a good idea to also feed them at least twice a week with plankton, finely minced seafood and filter feeder foods.

Favia and Favites Brain Coral

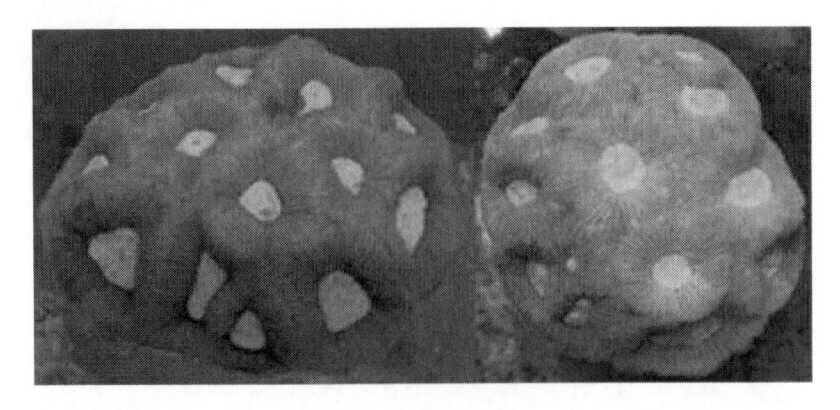

Favites Brain Coral

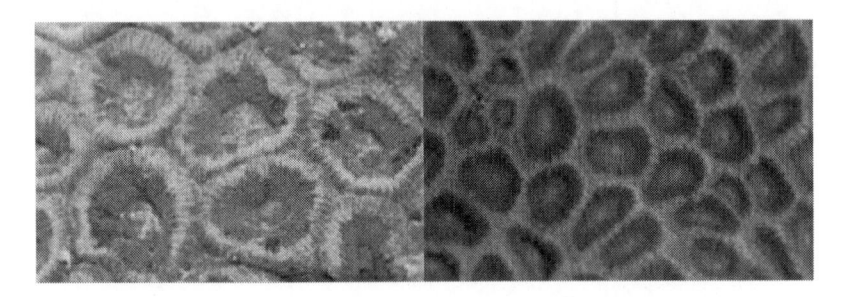

Favia Brain Corals - two of its many colors

NOTE: The picture on the left clearly exhibits the space between the walls around each polyp, a main difference in Favia Brain Coral and Favites Brain Coral.

 Favia and Favites Brain Coral have similar requirements but look slightly different from each other. They both normally have thick dome- or round-shaped skeletons. They are found in bright solid colors like green and orange as well as more muted colors like yellow, brown, cream and tan. Each coral can also have several colors where the polyp's dividing walls can be one color and the center between the walls another.
 Favia Coral have individual skeletal walls or ridges surrounding each polyp with space between the walls of other polyps. Favites

Corals have common skeletal walls shared by surrounding polyps. During the day their tissue expands to cover their skeleton which makes it difficult to tell whether you are looking at a Favia Coral or a Favites Coral. At night when the tissue deflates it is easy to see the difference.

Favites Brain Coral likes moderate to intense lighting along with moderate turbulent water movement. These corals can be placed at almost every level in an aquarium as long as there is at least moderate intensity light available.

Favia and Favites Brain Coral have long sweeper tentacles which appear at night and these corals should be placed at least six inches from other corals and sessile invertebrates.

They both have zooxanthellae in their tissue from which they receive most of their nutrients. They also have feeder tentacles which appear around each polyp after the lights go out. They will eat plankton, mysis shrimp, and prepared fish foods of raw minced seafood. Feed these corals at least once a week while their tentacles are out.

Euphyllia

The Euphyllia family has some of the most beautiful hardy corals with long, flowing polyps. Euphyllia's common names such as Hammer Coral (Euphyllia ancora) come from the shape of their polyps.

Euphyllia coral polyps are almost always fully extended during the day. Sometimes clown fish will host in their long tentacles if there is not an anemone present. When this happens, the coral will often retract its tentacles at first but over a few days will extend them like normal.

The majority of Euphyllia species prefer slow to moderate, intermittent water current. Water flow should keep tentacles lightly moving and fast enough to keep detritus for settling on them. If the water current is too powerful the tentacles will not fully expand.

Most Euphyllia need moderate light. If your reef has high intensity lighting, place the new coral low and move it up slowly over several weeks. When the polyps are fully extended is a good indicator that a coral is properly placed. Euphyllia have long sweeper tentacles with powerful stinging cells. Give these corals about six inches of room in all directions. Once the best location for a coral is determined, reef epoxy can be used to attach it to the live rock.

When handling Euphyllia never remove it from the water while its polyps are extended. It has a sharp skeleton surrounding the polyp that can tear it.

Under ideal lighting Euphyllia species do not need to be fed. They can be fed to increase growth rate by target feeding small mysis shrimp, minced squid, bits of fish, etc.

Euphyllia species (especially branching) colonies can grow quite large, often outgrowing their space. Fortunately branching species are easy to trim by either cutting or breaking a group of branches from the colony. They can now be moved to a new location or moved to another aquarium. Here are some great Euphyllia species

Frogspawn Coral (Euphyllia paradivisa)

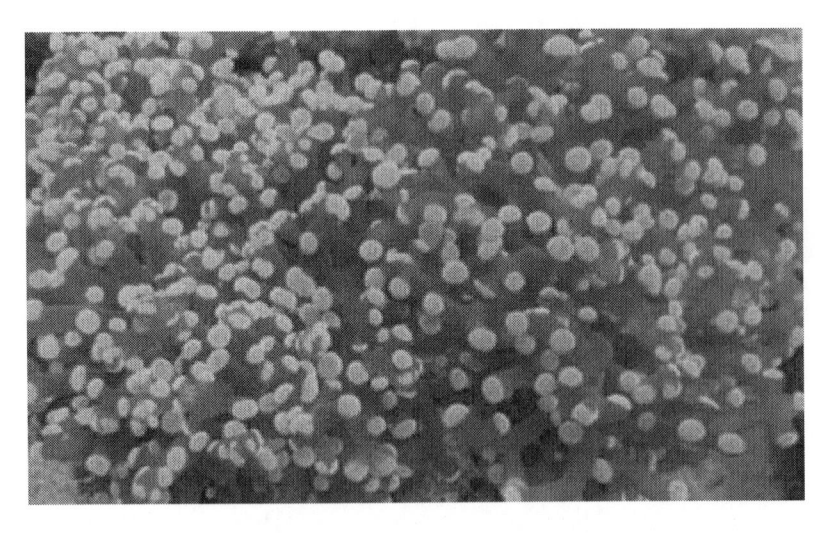

Close-up Frogspawn Coral

Frogspawn Corals look like a mass of frog eggs on the end of tan branching stalks. It has long tentacles ending with multiple knob-tipped branches. The tentacles are normally bright green or some shade of brown with the knob tips being a white, pink, green, cream or lavender color.

Hammer or Anchor Coral (Euphyllia ancora)

Green Hammer Coral

Hammer Coral has long tentacles with anchor-shaped, C-shaped or sausage-shaped tips. The tentacles extend out of the top of a curving skeleton described as wall-like, giving it its common name of a Wall Hammer. This also keeps it from being confused with the Branching Hammer Coral (Euphyllia parancora.)

Hammer Coral tentacles are normally a shade of brown or bright green with the tentacle tips often a lighter shade or even a different color. They may be a light color of pink, orange, green or blue.

Hammer Coral, Branching (Euphyllia parancora)

Branching Hammer Coral

Branching Hammer Coral has long tentacles with anchor-shaped or T-shaped tips. The tentacles extend from the end of each hard skeletal branch. Branching Hammer Coral tentacles are usually green, shades of brown with the tips of yellow or bright green tips.

Torch Coral (Euphyllia glabrescens)

Torch Coral

Torch Coral has beautiful long flowing polyps with rounded tips. Their tips are not as fancy as the hammer corals but they are very elegant and just as relaxing to watch as they flow in the water currents. The tentacles extend from the end of each hard skeletal branch and are usually green or brown with yellow or light color tips.

Pagoda Cup Coral (Turbinaria peltata)

Pagoda Cup with polyps mostly withdrawn and on right polyps closed

Pagoda Cup is a good beginner coral since it is hardy, peaceful and easy to care for. It is occasionally sold in a concave shape which can resemble a cup; you may also find it in other shapes including upright branching and columns. Pagoda Cup has large frilly yellow, brown, green, or gray polyps which cover the top surface of the coral.

Pagoda Cup is a slow, steady grower and will not bother other corals placed close to it. It needs a medium flow of water to help remove wastes combined with moderate lighting. It does well in the bottom half of the aquarium.

This coral uses large polyps to capture foods such as brine shrimp or plankton.

Plate Coral (Fungia sp.)

Orange and green with red Plate Coral

Plate Corals are great for beginners because they are easy to care for. Round like a plate or disc, it has a single mouth surrounded by short tentacles. They are available in tan, bright purple, green, orange and more.

Plate Corals should be placed directly on the sand away from other corals so it does not sting them. Leave plenty of room around this coral because it will swell up to catch food particles, usually at night. It can also move several inches a day across the sand.

Plate Corals are hardy and do well in moderate to high intensity light. They like low to medium turbulent water flow.

They obtain most of their nutrients from their internal zooxanthellae, depending on how much light they receive. It is beneficial to feed this coral at least once a week. They have a surprisingly large mouth and eat meaty foods like mysis shrimp, brine shrimp or other chopped raw seafood. The food can be placed directly on the coral. They should be fed when their tentacles are fully extended usually after the lights go out.

Because Plate Coral lies directly on the sand, hermit crabs and shrimp and even some fish may try to steal its food.

Small Polyp Stony (SPS) Corals

SPS Corals are something to look forward to keeping in the future. These corals take more care and coral keeping knowledge than Soft Corals. Their beauty makes them desirable, but they are not considered a beginner coral for the reasons discussed below.

Acropora Coral

The most breath-taking reef you will ever see is an established aquarium stocked with a variety of Acropora Corals. These corals are for experienced coral keepers who have learned to keep excellent water quality and they do best in established aquariums.

Acropora Coral are fast growers and are the largest contributors building our ocean reefs. These corals are available in numerous shapes, including branching, bushy, columns, clusters, fingers, ridges, table and more. Acropora Coral are found in some of the most vibrantly intense reds, blues, greens, purples, pinks, yellows, etc., and are thus worth learning about.

Acroporas need intense light and should be placed in the top third of the aquarium. They need high, variable and turbulent water flow to remove detritus build up; detritus often leads to dying tissue or skin if not removed from this gorgeous coral. Once this skin is gone, algae will grow in the dead area, slowly spreading to eat away at healthy tissue.

They are easy to propagate by cleanly cutting off a single branch and attaching it to a coral plug or a piece of rock. Acropora Corals are relatively peaceful towards other SPS type corals. They can, however, be stung by aggressive LPS corals, especially ones with sweeper tentacles.

Acropora corals get the majority of their nutrients from their zooxanthellae and also should be fed tiny zooplankton like rotifers, copepods and they will also eat oyster eggs, phytoplankton and micro prepared coral foods.

Birdsnest Coral (Seriatopora hystrix)

Pink Birdsnest Coral

Birdsnest Coral are beautiful with their thin, intertwining branches and pointed tips. They come in several colors, including pink, green, brown or orange.

These corals have thin, fragile branches which are easy to break while cleaning the aquarium. Should you happen to break off some of this delicate coral, use the broken branch or frag to start a new colony.

This peaceful coral requires moderate to strong indirect water flow, preferably with alternating water current. Do not blow water directly on the coral. Good water flow may keep algae from growing on the branches and tips.

Birdsnest Coral, like all SPS, need bright intense light. Place them in the upper half of the rockwork according to light intensity. Since they grow rather quickly, they need to be placed away from aggressive corals.

Though they get most of their nutrients from Zooxanthellae; feed them fine filter feeder food or tiny plankton weekly.

Montipora Capricornis (Montipora capricornis)

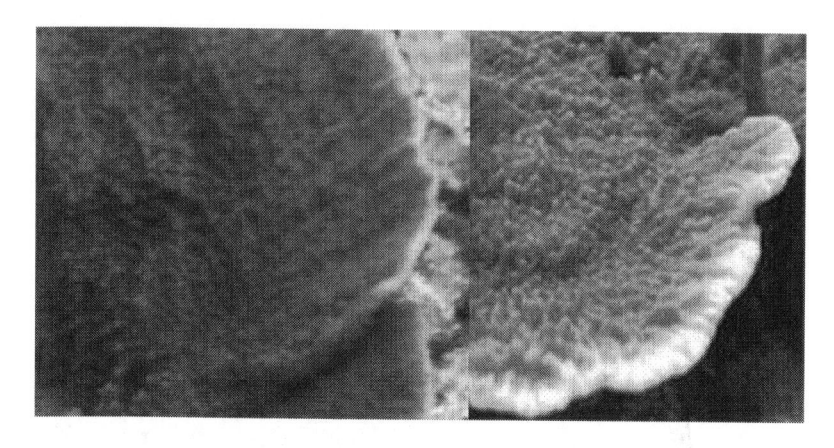

Montipora Capricornis

Montipora Capricornis is a one of the easier SPS corals to grow. It has a velvety appearance when its small polyps are opened; it is available in bold colors like orange, red, purple and green.

This encrusting coral can take on many shapes. One of the most beautiful shapes is spiraling with a leaf-like pattern. These leafy varieties are delicate and care must be taken when cleaning around them not to snap off a leaf. If a leaf is knocked off it can be reattached using a two part reef epoxy, back to the original colony or attached somewhere on the rockwork to start a new colony. New colonies can also be started by cutting or trimming the coral and attach it to a piece of rock or a reef plug.

Montipora Capricornis are relatively fast growers. There is usually a color difference between the new growth and the established coral. For example the red Montipora Capricornis has a bright white edge displaying new growth.

This coral needs medium to strong light and should be placed in the upper half of the aquarium. Ensure it has moderate to strong flow of turbulent water. This peaceful coral can easily get damaged by more aggressive stinging corals. It eats tiny zooplankton and commercial filter feeder foods as well as gets most of its nutrients from its photosynthesis zooxanthellae.

Montipora digitata (Montipora digitata)

Purple Montipora digitata

Montipora digitata is a branching coral with a fuzzy appearance; it is found in vivid colors. The fuzzy appearance appears when small polyps are extended.

Montipora digitata is peaceful, hardy, a fairly fast grower found in bright green, intense purple, orange or tan. This Montipora, unlike the encrusting or whirling leaves type, grows more like tree branches. Sometimes branches are merged together and the shapes of the branches are influenced by water flow, lighting and placement in the reef. The ends of the branches are rounded.

The Montipora digitata needs moderate fluctuating water currents combined with medium to high intensity light. It should be placed in the upper half of the reef.

This coral receives most of its nutrients through photosynthetic zooxanthellae and will also benefit from tiny zooplankton and commercial filter feeder foods.

Stylophora Coral (Stylophora spp.)

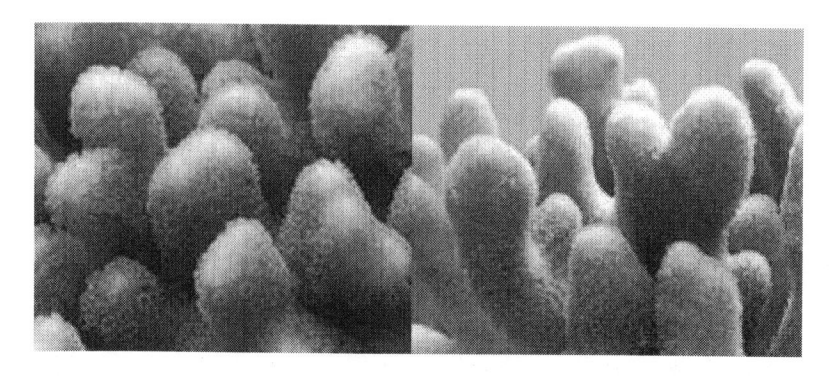

Stylophora Corals

Stylophora Coral is unique with its thick, flattened branches with rounded edges and round blunt tips. This coral is hardy but is for experienced hobbyists and well established reefs.

Available in beautiful pinks, greens and purples, Stylophora Coral does best in moderate to bright light; it should be placed in the upper half of an aquarium. It also requires moderate to strong turbulent water flow.

Regularly feed this coral zooplankton or other micro filter feeder foods; most nutrients are obtained from photosynthetic algae.

Conclusion

SPS, LPS and Soft Corals have many different requirements and defenses which need to be taken into consideration before mixing corals. A reef aquarium with only SPS, LPS or Soft Corals is easiest to keep and it is possible to successfully mix these different groups of corals in the same aquarium. It will take some placement planning and research on each coral to ensure their needs are met. To increase chances of success, choose less aggressive corals, leave plenty of space between them and use - and regularly change - activated filter carbon.

Once established, most corals are hardy as long as their needs are met and they are not being bothered by tank mates. Even in an established reef there is some flexibility: the majority of corals can be moved to different spots, trimmed or completely removed from a reef and replaced by another coral.

Bringing Your New Corals Home

Acclimation Method

1. Turn off the aquarium light to avoid stressing the corals and dim room lights.

2. Float sealed bag of corals in the aquarium or sump water for 15 to 30 minutes. The salesperson should have filled at least half the bag with air, enabling the bag to float in your aquarium. Floating the bag allows the water in the bag to gradually adjust to the same temperature as the aquarium water.

3. Put a clean, nontoxic or food-grade container or bucket in front of the aquarium. The number and size of the corals you are adding to your aquarium determines the size of the bucket you will need. Generally a three to five gallon container will do.

NOTE: when acclimating a new coral make sure you keep it in a separate container from fish and invertebrates that you acclimate at the same time.

4. Once the temperature of the water in the plastic bag is the same as the water in the aquarium, open the bag and pour the water into the bucket. Gently place the coral in the water you just poured. Hard coral needs to be carried by its stony part without touching the flesh. It is advisable to wear disposable sterile rubber gloves since some people are allergic to the toxins that corals release; gloves ensure that nothing on your hands affect the corals and can prevent being stung by aggressive corals. If there is not enough water to cover the corals,

place something under one side of the bucket to make a pocket of deep water inside.

> *NOTE: This slow acclimation method will slowly raise the ph; drip acclimation alters the bucket water to match the aquarium water parameters. Remember to always acclimate in a shaded or dark area as corals are sensitive to sudden light changes.*

5. Add an ammonia neutralizing product to the bucket of water with the corals. There are several products available at aquarium stores which will quickly neutralize ammonia.

6. Start a siphon to slowly drip water from your aquarium into the container. The siphon is a section of airline tubing, generally four to six feet long, with an adjustable valve on one end.

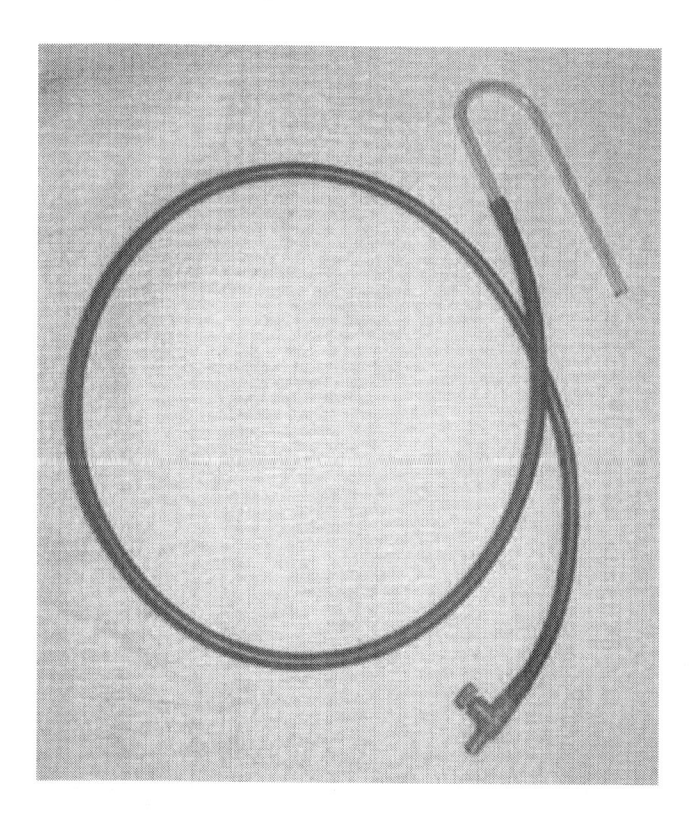

Drip line with plastic u-shape pipe to hang on rim of aquarium, airline tubing and valve

Place the end of the tubing without the valve in your aquarium; suck on the valve end to begin water flow. Place the tubing in the bucket and slowly open and close the valve until it drips two to four drops per second.

7. Cover the bucket to keep corals in the dark.

8. When the water in the bucket has doubled, dip out about half of the water and discard.

9. Let the water level double again.

10. Test the pH of the water in the bucket. If it matches the water of the reef aquarium acclimation is complete. If not continue the drip method until pH of the bucket matches your reef.

11. Once acclimation is complete place corals in a clean container with a premixed commercial coral dip. Follow the manufacturer's directions on the coral dip; remove the desired amount of water from your reef and mix it with the recommended dip dosage. Gently place acclimated corals into this container for the manufacturer's specified time, usually ten to fifteen minutes. Every few minutes, use a turkey baster to gently blast water at the corals to help circulate the water as well as to knock most pests off the coral.

11. Next, transfer the coral to the aquarium. Some dips recommend a final rinsing of the coral in new water from your aquarium. Place the coral in the lower to middle of your aquarium for the first week to allow the coral to slowly adjust to the intensity of the reef light. After the first week, move the coral to a more ideal spot in your aquarium.

12. Add premixed saltwater to the aquarium to replace the water that was removed during the acclimation process.

NOTE: Corals may take several hours or days to fully inflate and extend their tentacles.

Follow these tips as well:

TIPS:

Feed a small amount of food to help distract the original tank inhabitants from picking on the new corals.

Leave the aquarium light off for a few hours to give corals a chance to acclimate

Watch new corals for territorial disputes, not inflating or not extending tentacles.

Move coral to a new location if you think another coral is irritating it.

Chapter 8

How and What to Feed Fish, Invertebrates and Corals

Feeding Fish

Feeding

After good water quality, feeding is probably the next most important aspect in keeping fish healthy. There are an overwhelming number of different fish foods available including frozen, dry, freeze-dried and live foods. It is important to become acquainted with the types of food a fish requires before purchasing the fish (does it require high protein or extra vegetable matter?) It is best to feed frozen food as a staple and use dry foods to supplement. The key to keeping fish healthy and ensuring that they are getting a complete diet is to feed a variety of foods and/or add vitamins to the food.

Frozen Foods

There are countless frozen fish foods on the market today including specialty foods for particular species, foods that are blended for herbivores, carnivores, and omnivores. They are designed to copy the diversity of food that fish would get in the wild. Most blended foods consist primarily of various seafood and algae. Some manufacturers add color enhancers and vitamins. Blended foods are ideal for everyday feeding.

Prepared frozen fish food in easy pop-out cubes for carnivores, omnivores and herbivores

Specialty foods include krill, mysis shrimp, squid, mussels and plankton, to name a few. Your fish are the best indicators of what foods they like and do not like. It is best to use a wide variety to ensure a balanced and nutritious diet.

Frozen foods, stored properly, are about as close to fresh food as you can get. Some manufacturers use a gel binder to keep the food from falling apart once it defrosts. Other foods immediately begin to fall apart as they hit the water. Foods without a gel binder work well for smaller fish because they fall apart; larger fish prefer larger chunks and a gel binder will help keep the food together to keep them happy.

TIP: Thaw frozen food in RO/DI water to remove phosphates and other possible preservatives. Then, pour defrosted food through a fine fish net before feeding it to your fish. A few frozen food manufacturers rinse their foods prior to mixing and freezing. Some of these pre-rinsed foods have microparticles to feed corals and should not be rinsed again or fine particles will be removed.

Dry Foods

There have been many advances in dry foods to increase the nutritional value and keep vitamins from oxidizing. Remember, variety is the spice of life. While frozen is best as a main staple food, there are many excellent dry foods that can be added as supplements to increase the nutritional value of their diets. Again, your fish will let you know what they like.

To keep dry foods fresh, purchase small size containers. It is usually cheaper to buy bulk size containers of food but, from a freshness and nutritional standpoint, it is best to buy enough food to last 1 to 2 months.

Freeze Dried Foods

Freeze-dried foods are great supplements. The best feature about this type of food is its ability to soak up vitamins and trace elements - especially helpful when you have sick fish. Set the freeze-dried food of choice, such as freeze-dried krill, into a bowl and pour liquid fish vitamins over it. After a few minutes, the vitamins will soak into the food.

Algae Sheets

Many fish such as tangs, rabbit fish and most angels spend their days grazing the live rock looking for algae or seaweed. When an algae is in short supply or you want to supplement your fishes' diets, try algae sheets. These sheets are made of dried seaweed and are especially nutritious for fish. A product called a lettuce clip is available to hold the algae sheet in place via a suction cup or magnet. Place a sheet or strip of dried seaweed in the clip and attach the suction cup against the inside wall of the aquarium.

Seaweed and clip attached to front glass of aquarium

Feed algae strips daily if you have several herbivores and very little existing algae in your aquarium. Otherwise, feed a couple of times a week as a supplement. If the fish devour the algae sheet within the first few minutes, you can add all or part of another. The algae sheet will eventually decompose if not eaten.

TIPS: If you have excess algae growing on your live rock, you may want to reduce the number of algae sheets you feed to force your herbivore(s) to graze naturally on the algae growing in the aquarium.

Live Foods

Saltwater live foods such as brine shrimp (sea monkeys) and copepods (small crustaceans) will be quickly consumed by your fish. Copepods and brine shrimp are very small and are therefore perfect for small fish and finicky eaters.

Brine shrimp is often sold in too large a quantity to use in one feeding and you may need to set up a small holding tank to keep the excess. Copepods come in a bottle or container which can be used for storing. Depending on the type of copepod they may need to be refrigerated; some may be kept at room temperature.

Copepods can also be added to a refugium to establish a colony. Some copepods will be sucked up by the return water pump and wind up as food for your fish, invertebrates and corals. Others, hopefully, will remain in the refugium, grow and reproduce. Once a colony is established, use a fine mesh fish net to catch some of the larger copepods and feed to your fish.

Suggestions for Fussy Eaters

Some fish are finicky eaters or do not recognize food and must be enticed into eating something different from what they found in the wild. Try different types of foods; or add an appetite stimulator to encourage fish to eat. Many fish are used to eating live foods; you may want to try live brine shrimp and copepods.

Feeding Made Simple

It seems like feeding fish would be simple, but sometimes it takes a little forethought to make certain everyone gets a fair chance at the food. The real trick to successful feeding is to feed each fish well without over feeding the aquarium. You can accomplish this by paying close attention to the fish while you drop food into the water. Add a small amount of food and watch; if the fish eat it all, add more. Food should be consumed before hitting the bottom of the aquarium unless you are aiming to feed crabs or shrimp. If any food is left uneaten, remove it and feed less next time.

Try to feed fish around the same time every day. It is better to give your fish small amounts several times throughout the day rather than a large amount once a day. If there is extra food after fish have stopped eating, net it out or use a siphon to remove it. Thaw frozen food before feeding. Food that is prepared in a gelatinous base can be mashed into pieces for smaller fish after it is thawed.

Feeding Coral

Corals are either non-photosynthetic and must acquire all their food from surrounding saltwater or photosynthetic which obtain their food in many ways. One way is through symbiotic algae (zooxanthellae) living in the tissue of coral polyps. Through photosynthesis, zooxanthellae creates nutrients for itself and its host coral. Corals also obtain food by actively catching and eating zooplankton, phytoplankton, bacterioplankton, etc. Another way corals obtain food is through the absorption of dissolved organic molecules and particulate organic material.

As you can see, photosynthetic corals have an assortment of feeding choices. This has caused much confusion for hobbyist, should they feed their corals or let them survive on good light alone.

There are many reefs with healthy populations of beautiful photosynthetic corals which have never been supplemented with coral foods. Even though the only nutrient supplied by zooxanthellae is carbohydrates which are sugar and starches. But for corals to grow and exist they require vitamins, lipids, proteins and more. They acquire most of these nutrients through uneaten fish food, fish waste, bacteria, etc.

This leads to the question, will corals thrive or simply survive if they are not fed food they would normally consume in nature?

There are corals like Zoanthids, which grow and multiply in a reef aquarium without additional food, as long as there is a reasonable fish population. On the other hand, there are also photosynthetic corals that do not do well unless they are supplemented with coral food regularly. With this said most corals fed on a regular basis will grow faster and appear healthier than their not-supplemented counterparts.

There is a vast array of corals with diets varying from microscopic algae to corals that eat small fish and chunks of raw seafood. Let's take a close look at some ideal foods for our coral friends.

Coral Foods

Plankton is a universal name for phytoplankton and zooplankton.

Phytoplankton is nutrient-packed microscopic algae. This is not one type of algae but a large group of microalgae made up of dinoflagellates and diatoms. In the ocean, phytoplankton provides food for a wide assortment of sea creatures including clams, feather dusters, corals, zooplankton and more.

Zooplankton is a plethora of microscopic to small aquatic animals. These include animals which will remain zooplankton their entire life (copepods and brine shrimp) as well as animals which are considered zooplankton during only a part of their lives (the larvae stage of most fish, snails and clams.) Some zooplankton frequently used to feed corals are rotifers, copepods, brine shrimp and mysis shrimp.

Frozen coral foods are readily available from aquarium and pet stores. They include meaty foods like brine shrimp, chopped clams, chopped shrimp, cyclops, krill, mysis shrimp, silversides (small whole fish), rotifers, zooplankton and more. There are also frozen coral foods which are a blend of phytoplankton and tiny zooplankton. Many of the frozen foods mentioned are also used to feed invertebrates and fish.

Some frozen foods are a combination of all kinds of foods in a single package designed to feed corals, fish and invertebrates. This food blankets the water with an assortment of different-sized particles.

Liquid foods include live foods, preserved (once alive) and specialty blends. Live food and most preserved food contain critters like phytoplankton, copepods, oyster eggs and rotifers. Liquid specialty blends include foods which replicate natural marine snow in the ocean to an assortment of other combinations of food and matter for filter feeders.

Dry coral foods include dried phytoplankton, zooplankton, krill and lots of other seafood. There are also proprietary coral food blends.

Coral Feeding Tips

The best time to Feed

In the ocean, corals normally extend their tentacles and polyps at night to capture prey when the level of plankton in the water column is the highest. In a home aquarium most corals will also extend their feeding tentacles when the lights go out. Over time, most corals will learn to extend their polyps and eat during the day when food is present in the water. Before feeding your corals, feed your fish. Feeding fish a thawed frozen food will normally stimulate corals to begin to extend their feeding tentacles.

Powerheads or Circulation Pumps

Before feeding corals, turn off the powerheads or circulation pump and main return pump and wait for the aquarium to become still. When feeding without a current the food can fall onto the corals so that its tentacles can grab it. Live foods like copepods can easily be captured. Leave the pumps off for fifteen minutes to an hour before turning them back on.

Depending on your circulation system, once the corals get in the habit of capturing food you may be able to leave powerheads running while feeding. Most corals should be able to capture their food. The return pump should stay off for at least fifteen minutes to an hour to allow corals to remove food from the water. Since most reefs use a mechanical filter (filter socks, for example) the food falling over the overflow box gets trapped in it. This is obviously dependent on how large the food is and how small the pores are in the sock. Food trapped in socks will break down and produce nutrients to feed unwanted algae.

> *NOTE: A challenge can arise when you unplug your main pump with powerheads still circulating water - You may not notice the return pump is off! Make sure you leave a cabinet door open, use a timer or controller, or any other method as a reminder to turn the return pump back on.*

Protein Skimmer

Depending on your filtration system setup, it may be advantageous to turn off your protein skimmer when feeding for about two hours. A vacation timer allows you to turn off your skimmer for a specific time and automatically turns it back on, thus ensuring the skimmer does not get forgotten.

Protein skimmers do a great job of removing excess food when a reef is overfed.

Target feeding

Target feeding is a great way to control how much food goes into an aquarium. To target feed use a turkey baster, long medicine dropper or similar feeding apparatus and gently squirt food in the direction of the intended corals. The food can be liquid phytoplankton or zooplankton; mysis shrimp mixed with aquarium water or any other coral food in a liquid form or can be mixed with water.

To target feed an LPS coral (a Fungia or Lobophyllia, for instance) mix frozen mysis shrimp with a little aquarium water. Once the shrimp has thawed, slurp the mixture up with a turkey baster. Staying several inches away from the coral, gently squirt some of the shrimp so they land on the coral. The tentacles will sense the food, capture it and within a short time you can see the food traveling to the mouth, and watch it be slowly drawn in. This entire process just takes a few minutes.

General Coral Food Suggestions

- Most Soft Corals eat phytoplankton, brine shrimp, rotifers and oyster eggs.
- Most Polyps like Zoanthids eat phytoplankton, rotifers, copepods, and oyster eggs.
- Most Large Polyp Stony Coral will eat brine shrimp, phytoplankton, rotifers, copepods, oyster eggs, silversides, krill, mysis shrimp and other chopped raw seafood.
- Small Polyp Stony Corals eat zooplankton such as rotifers and copepods. They will also eat oyster eggs and phytoplankton.
- Non-Photosynthetic Corals eat phytoplankton, rotifers, copepods, mysis shrimp and oyster eggs.

Words to the Wise

The down side to feeding corals is that if all the food is not being eaten by the corals, nutrients can build up, thus reducing water quality, causing an algae explosion. A good protein skimmer, refugium, activated carbon and regular water changes help keep ideal water quality with proper feeding.

If your reef already has an algae problem without feeding your corals it is best to wait until your algae is under control before attempting to feed them, or only target-feed corals very lightly.

Conclusion

The most important part of keeping most corals healthy is good water quality, ideal light and regular feedings with the right foods. Healthy, growing corals are a good indication you are feeding enough. Your best choice of coral food is live, preserved or frozen foods.

Feeding Invertebrates

In a reef aquarium **most crabs, shrimp and snails** are added as part of a cleanup crew. These foragers generally find plenty of food to eat. If they require additional food or you have non-cleanup animals go to Invertebrates are Beneficial and Fun to find individual species recommendations.

Feather Dusters and Coco Worms eat phytoplankton, fine detritus from the water, oyster eggs, prepared liquid and frozen foods designed and labeled specifically for filter feeders. A turkey baster may be used to lightly blow food into the current towards the crown. If you try to blow food directly at the crown it will retract into its tube and will not eat.

Small to medium-size Brittle Stars and Serpent Stars are carnivores, making them excellent scavengers of detritus and uneaten meaty fish food.

Sand Sifting Sea Stars are omnivores. They eat detritus, small crustacean, microfauna (microscopic animals) and uneaten foods. In cleaner aquariums their diet can be supplemented with a small amount of fish food such as mysis shrimp. Feed them at night when the fish are resting.

Tridacna Clams have symbiotic algae called zooxanthellae which provide most of the food and nutrients. Tridacna Clams are filter feeders and can help maintain good water quality by absorbing nitrates and other organics. Their diet can also be supplemented with phytoplankton and oyster eggs.

Most Sea Urchins are great at eating many types of algae in a reef including coralline algae. They will also eat Nori seaweed, foods high in spirulina, kelp and other forms of algae.

Anemones have symbiotic algae (zooxanthellae) living in their tissue which, through photosynthesis, create nutrients. They will eat silversides (small whole fish) and chopped raw seafood like squid, krill, shrimp and fish.

Overfeeding

Overfeeding can cause water quality problems! In addition, uneaten, decaying food becomes food for unwanted algae such as filamentous and red slime algae (Cyanobacteria.)

If an aquarium has been overfed and you are concerned, test the water for ammonia. Test the water the day of and day after the incident. Excess food can be siphoned out of the aquarium (explained in How to Care for a Reef) and fresh saltwater replenished. If the ammonia level is high, do a significant water change of at least 25%. Test the levels later that day or the next day. The ammonia levels on an established aquarium will generally go back to zero within a short period of time.

Protein skimmers are excellent at removing dissolved organic wastes. Activated filter carbon will also help by adsorbing dissolved organic wastes from the water and will eliminate foul odors caused by decaying food.

Chapter 9

Setting Up a Saltwater Quarantine Tank

It is always a good idea to quarantine newly purchased saltwater fish rather than adding them directly from the store to an established aquarium. Many hobbyists skip this process, and some get lucky, but you should quarantine all new fish for at least three weeks before transferring them to their display aquarium. Most pet and aquarium stores do not have the space or time to quarantine fish.

FREE BONUS: Claim your FREE copy of "How You Can Select Healthy Fish, Like the Experts" at http://9nl.be/FreeReefBonuses

Since the majority of saltwater fish are collected from the ocean, they endure a tremendous amount of stress while being snatched from their familiar surroundings, packed in plastic bags, stuffed in dark boxes and flown halfway around the world. They need time to recuperate, heal and get used to aquarium living.

The larger problem is if a sick fish goes into your reef it can infect your existing fish. What makes it worse it is very difficult to catch even a sick fish out of a reef packed with lots of rockwork. Save yourself some stress and quarantine all new fish.

Benefits of a Quarantine Aquarium

A quarantine aquarium, usually smaller than the show aquarium, is a place to acclimate new fish. Use it as a treatment or hospital aquarium for sick fish, a holding tank for aggressive fish, and even a recovery place for injured fish. Many of the supplies needed for this aquarium are similar to those needed for your show aquarium. Following is a list of equipment to build a quarantine tank along with necessary test kits.

Supplies and Equipment Needed

- 10 to 29 gallon aquarium - to keep fish up to five inches
- Filter - sponge filter or hang-on filter
- Submersible heater
- Thermometer
- Top - glass or plastic
- Light
- Plastic decorations or PVC pipe
- Hydrometer
- Net
- Siphon hose or gravel vacuum

Testing Supplies

- Hydrometer
- High range pH test kit
- Ammonia test kit
- Nitrite test kit
- Copper test kit

Eight Steps to Setting Up a Quarantine Tank

1. Rinse the aquarium with water only. If you have used this aquarium before, consider sterilizing it; use a light bleach solution as described later.

2. Place the aquarium on a stand or solid flat surface that can support its weight.

3. Attach a filter. Use a sponge filter or, preferably, a hang-on filter. Replace any cartridges with filter floss or a filter pad when medicating. Activated carbon found inside factory cartridges will remove most medications.

4. Attach a heater to the inside back of the aquarium, on the side opposite from the filter. Set the temperature between 78 and 80 degrees Fahrenheit.

5. Fill the aquarium with premix RO or RO/DI water. The water in the quarantine tank should have the same specific gravity and pH parameters as in your display aquarium. The temperature may be a little warmer than the show aquarium, though, as this will help speed up parasite cycles and/or diseases if you are treating fish.

6. Once the aquarium is full of water, turn on the filter. After about ten minutes, plug in the heater.

7. Place artificial plastic decorations throughout the aquarium.

8. Place a top and light on the aquarium. If possible, let the quarantine aquarium run for 24 hours to ensure the heater and filter are working properly. Otherwise, keep a close eye on the temperature and water movement.

Quarantine aquarium: filter, heater, light and decoration

Decorating a Quarantine Aquarium

Decorations in quarantine are very important. Decorations in a quarantine aquarium are not for our aesthetic enjoyment but they are there to provide fish with places to hide from us, to feel more secure and, overall, to have a quicker and healthier acclimation. Make sure there are enough hiding spots for all fish. Larger fish will naturally need larger decorations to feel comfortable.

Decorations should be plastic: PVC pipes, elbows or tees large enough for the fish to swim inside of are perfect; molded decorations are also fine. Many new hobbyists errantly use dead coral skeletons and shells to make the fish feel at home since those are things found in its natural habitat. **DO NOT use them**.

Sand or gravel is also not recommended for a quarantine aquarium. Dead coral skeletons, shells, crushed coral and aragonite (substrates) absorb copper and may absorb medications. Using coral of any size, or aragonite in a quarantine tank increases the amount of medication needed to dose the aquarium and/or the frequency that dosing is required. In addition, since a quarantine tank sometimes doubles as a treatment or "hospital" tank, it is a good idea to streamline what you use so that the décor can be used for either.

Add plastic or silk plants to finish create a safe-feeling habitat for your new fish.

Biological Filtration

Hospital or quarantine aquariums cycle like any other aquarium when they are first set up. Because these tanks are for new or sick fish, it is important to keep ammonia and nitrite levels in check so as not to further traumatize the already stressed fish.

One option is to keep a quarantine or hospital aquarium running all the time with some small or inexpensive fish in it. Another option is to keep a sponge or other easily removed media in your display aquarium sump on which to grow beneficial bacteria. This media is then ready to use in your hospital aquarium at a moment's notice. When you set up a quarantine aquarium, add the colonized media to the filter to help keep ammonia and nitrite levels from rising to toxic levels.

NOTE: Many antibiotics kill beneficial bacteria. Should fish require treatment with antibiotics it may be best to save the colonized media for another time.

If you must treat your fish with antibiotics, or if you do not have or simply choose not to use colonized media, be sure to closely monitor ammonia and nitrite levels and change water as often as is needed to keep them low or nonexistent. Test water daily, change water often, and you can still be successful.

Adding Fish

Take a few minutes to set a mood for moving fish. Turn off the aquarium light and dim the room lights. Make sure to acclimate (following acclimation methods in "Bringing Your New Fish Home" in Chapter 5) fish before releasing them into the quarantine aquarium. The size of the aquarium determines how many fish it can house together. Once you release the fish, let them relax for the first few hours or overnight before turning on the light. Turn the light on during the day and off at night. Turning the light on and off at the same time each day is another way to ease stress on tank inhabitants (use an appliance timer).

Feed fish a variety of foods lightly, twice a day. As always, feed only what your fish will eat without any food landing on the bottom of the aquarium. If you happen to overfeed, net or siphon out any extra food immediately.

Vitamins

Adding vitamins to fish food is a good idea to aid ailing fish and boost the immune systems of healthy fish.

Medications

Medications are a choice. You may wait and observe fish for any stressful signs without adding medications or you may add medication immediately. In any case, to strengthen the immune systems of fish, make sure water quality remains consistent.

Watching Ammonia and Nitrite Levels

Test water daily. The main levels of concern are ammonia and nitrite; these levels should remain at zero or very close to zero. Change water if they rise. Generally you would remove 25% to 50% of the water in the tank and refill it with clean saltwater of the same salinity, temperature and pH.

With the many different sized aquariums that can be used, the differing numbers and sizes of fish kept as well as varying feeding amounts, there are no hard, fast rules on how often to change water in a quarantine or hospital aquarium. The best indicator is to test water and watch the fish for signs of stress. Perform water changes with a gravel siphon (vacuum) or a section of 5/8" to 3/4" flexible tubing. Make sure you siphon any waste from the bottom of the aquarium.

Specific Gravity and pH Tests

Another level to watch is specific gravity. When water evaporates, pour only fresh RO water back into the aquarium. During water changes make sure specific gravity and temperature are constant. The final test is pH; make sure it reads between 8.1 and 8.3. If pH dips below 8.1, add a buffer to raise it slowly back up. Other tests may be required depending on use of medications. Unless the tank has been set up for a long time, there should be little reason to worry about nitrate levels.

When to Move Quarantine Fish to the Display Aquarium

If after three weeks a fish eats well and appears to be healthy, it is ready to move to your display aquarium. Follow the procedure to acclimate fish (see "Bringing Your New Fish Home" in Chapter 5).

Before you move the new fish, feed the fish in your display aquarium. Also, turn the light off for a few hours to calm tank inhabitants and help keep them from harassing new arrivals.

Medicating Sick or Wounded Fish

Try never to put medications into your reef aquarium.

If the aquarium is not already set up, fill the hospital tank halfway with water from your display aquarium and the rest with mixed saltwater of the same salinity, temperature and pH to make the transfer less stressful on the patient.

If the aquarium is already set up, acclimate the fish by either using the drip method or by floating them in a bag and adding water slowly over time.

If a fish has torn fins, it will generally heal on its own; if there are wounds on the side of its body, it may be necessary to treat the water to keep any infections at bay.

When treating sick fish, a hospital tank is the best place to do it. As mentioned before, water quality has to be very good for these fish to get better. The key to healing sick and stressed fish is to get their immune systems up to speed and let the fish cure themselves.

Chapter 10

How to Care for a Reef

As with all living things, routine maintenance is required to keep fish, invertebrates, and corals healthy and a reef looking great. The best way to avoid stress and, ultimately, diseases is to keep the water in the aquarium in ideal condition. This entails regular water changes, siphoning (vacuuming) the substrate, changing filter media, etc. As you will see, not everything has to be done at once.

Daily

Not all maintenance has to do with getting your hands wet. Some of it is just plain fun! Feed your fish at least once each day (detailed feeding information in How and What to Feed Fish, Invertebrates and Corals.) Take a few minutes to observe your fish and watch them eat. Make sure they are all able to get food and learn their habits, so that you will be able to recognize what is normal for each fish. Check for clamped fins, white spots, labored breathing, abnormal hiding, etc. Also feed corals regularly and observe their health and eating habits.

Check the temperature and make sure it is between 76° and 78°. Salt never evaporates, so add salt-free RO or RO/DI water to your aquarium when the water level drops. Check to make sure your filter and pumps are working properly. Make certain that water is physically moving in your aquarium.

If the water is cloudy or smells bad test the ammonia and nitrite levels. Cloudy water could indicate that the fish have been overfed (it only takes overfeeding once to foul the water); it could also indicate that one (or more) of your fish is dead and decaying. If anything looks amiss, is it prudent to find the underlying reason so you can correct it.

Weekly

Algae is natural and overall helpful in an aquarium, but it is difficult to see through when it grows on the glass. Using an algae magnet (so you don't get your hands wet) clean the algae from the sides of the aquarium as it grows. It just takes a minute or two if you keep up with it regularly. Empty and clean the protein skimmer waste collection cup and rinse or change the mechanical filter media. (Mechanical filter media include socks, pads, and cartridges.)

Biweekly / Monthly

Some aquariums require partial biweekly water changes; others are good for once a month. Either way, water changes require some time. You will want to siphon or vacuum debris from the substrate and clean the filter and other equipment. Also, corals which have grown too large may need to be trimmed or fragged, which is actually cutting a piece of the coral off in order to start a new one.

Every 6 to 12 Months

Replace Light Bulbs

In a reef aquarium, fluorescent, compact fluorescent and metal halide bulbs should be replaced every 6 to 12 months depending on the lamp and ballast. Animals such as sea anemones and corals use light as a food source, so to keep these animals healthy change bulbs when recommended.

Replace UV Sterilizer Bulbs

UV sterilizer bulbs should be replaced every 6 to 12 months depending on the ballast. Over time, a UV bulb loses its intensity; it becomes ineffective in killing parasites, bacteria, fungi and algae.

Here is a list of some of the most pertinent equipment you will need in order to change water in and clean your aquarium:

Water change supplies
- Gravel vacuum (siphon)

- Algae scraper
- Algae magnet or sponge
- Salt mix
- Hydrometer
- Reverse osmosis water
- Aquarium glass cleaner
- Towels
- Fish net
- Turkey baster (used to blow debris off live rock)
- Clean bucket (used only for water changes)

Testing supplies
- Hydrometer
- pH test kit
- Ammonia test kit
- Nitrite test kit
- Nitrate test kit
- Calcium test kit
- Carbonate hardness test kit
- Optional test kits - phosphates, copper

15 Steps to Maintaining a Reef Aquarium

Step 1: Inspect Fish Health

Watch your fish. If they are ordinarily out and swimming around and are now hiding there could be a problem. Make sure their eyes are clear, they are not breathing heavily and the body and fins are clear of any abnormalities such as tears or chunks missing. For close inspection, use a magnifying glass. Observe corals ensure they are acting normal.

Step 2: Test the Water

- Use aquarium test kits to test ammonia, nitrite, nitrate, carbonate hardness.

- Ammonia and nitrite should read zero.
- Nitrate level should not to exceed 10 mg/L.
- Keep pH between 8.2 and 8.4.
- Carbonate hardness or alkalinity should be between 8 and 13 dkh.
- Keep Calcium level between 400 and 450 ppm.
- Use a hydrometer to test specific gravity or salinity. Specific gravity should be between 1.023 and 1.025.
- Check the aquarium temperature and ensure it is between 76° and 78° year round.

Step 3: Clean Algae from Interior Glass

Clean or scrape algae off the inside walls of the aquarium with a hand-held algae scraper, an algae pad on a stick or an algae magnet. Algae magnets are great because they keep your hands out of the aquarium. As you move the outside magnet around, the inside magnet scrapes off algae. Standard algae magnets are good for soft algae, but hard algae or coralline may require a scraper with a plastic or metal blade. A razor blade scraper may be used on glass aquariums, but be careful around silicone seals.

NOTE: Acrylic aquariums call for special tools to keep from scratching the surface.

Step 4: Clean Live Rock

Normally there is no need to scrub live rock clean. Fish and invertebrates like to graze the rocks for algae. Over time detritus and debris builds up on the rock. Use a turkey baster to blast water at the rocks blowing off the detritus and debris to the bottom of aquarium. You can also use a six to eight foot piece of flexible tubing 1/2" to 5/8" in diameter to siphon detritus from live rocks into a bucket. If you really want to scrub the live rock, use a small brush or toothbrush.

Step 5: Unplug Equipment

During the water change it is necessary to unplug or turn off the electrical equipment. Unplug or turn off the power strips that the protein skimmer water pump(s), return water pump and heater are plugged into. If the powerheads are attached close to the surface of the aquarium they will also need to be unplugged. If you have metal halide lights, turn them off and let them cool. The fixtures will be hot. Unplug everything except perhaps some light so that you can see what you are doing. To make servicing the aquarium easier, put all the equipment that needs to be unplugged on the same electrical power strip. This way you can quickly turn off the power and easily turn the power back on when you are finished.

Step 6: Vacuum Substrate and Remove Water

It is now time to clean the substrate. Place the large end of the gravel vacuum into the aquarium and the long flexible tube end into a bucket. Start the siphon by following the manufacturer's directions. The water should now be flowing into the bucket. Push the gravel vacuum into the sand to remove accumulated detritus and water at the same time. Try to vacuum as much of the substrate as possible. If water flows too quickly, pinch the flexible tubing to slow the water flow.

Gravel vacuum sand to remove detritus and water at the same time

Keep an eye on how much water you are removing. You can complete small water changes of 10 to 15% every other week, or change at least 25% once per month. If you have sand-sifting starfish or other invertebrates in the sand, take care not to injure them when vacuuming the substrate.

Step 7: Add Saltwater, Test and Add Additives

Using a hydrometer, test the specific gravity of your aquarium water. It should read between 1.023 and 1.025. If it reads too high, decrease it by adding less salt to the replacement water. If the salinity reads too low, simply mix replacement water to a slightly higher salinity. For example, if your aquarium water has specific gravity of 1.026, add replacement saltwater with a specific gravity of 1.022.

If you are using premixed saltwater you bought from a store to fill your aquarium then follow the premixed saltwater section directions. If you need to mix your own RO or RO/DI saltwater then go to the section below labeled mixing your own saltwater.

Premixed Saltwater

If you are using premix RO or RO/DI saltwater you purchased from the store it is still a good idea to run a few tests. Test the specific gravity, it should read between 1.023 and 1.025. If the specific gravity is too low, add more salt. If you add too much salt and the hydrometer reads over the target, remove some of the water and add fresh RO water.

Test pH and make sure it is between 8.2 and 8.4. If the pH is below 8.2, add a buffering agent to adjust it (information about pH can be found in Water Quality Explained in Chapter 4 .) The water should be around room temperature, though that may be a few degrees cooler then the aquarium. Since we are changing a small amount of water, the difference in temperature should not make a huge difference and will not make a significant change in the aquarium's water temperature. If the water is very cold, let it adjust to room temperature before beginning a water change.

Mixing Your Own Saltwater

If you have your own RO filter system, begin by filling a 5-gallon bucket or larger non-toxic container (preferably with wheels) with RO water. Next, add salt to the water. Follow the instructions on the salt mix, keeping in mind that a general rule is to add approximately one cup of salt to every two gallons of aquarium water.

After thoroughly mixing salt with the water in the bucket, use a hydrometer to test specific gravity. The specific gravity should read between 1.023 and 1.025. If the specific gravity is too low, add more salt. If you add too much salt and the hydrometer reads over the target, remove some of the water and add fresh RO water.

The RO filter system should have removed chlorine and/or chloramines; therefore a water conditioner is not necessary. Test pH and make sure it is between 8.2 and 8.4. If the pH is below 8.2, add a buffering agent to adjust it (information about pH can be found in Water Quality Explained in Chapter 4.)

Step 8: Adding Saltwater Back to the Aquarium

To replace water, just pour the premixed saltwater directly from the bucket or container into the aquarium; or use a water pump to return water to the aquarium. A submersible water pump attached to a 6-foot piece of flexible tubing is useful when changing large amounts of water. Pumping the water into the aquarium takes less muscle. If you are using a bucket, you will need to pour the water slowly onto one of the live rocks close to the water level or into the aquarium water. Fill the aquarium until the water level is just above the bottom of the aquarium's frame and water begins to flow over the overflow.

At this point you can either continue to add water to the aquarium to fill the Berlin sump in the cabinet or you can pour water directly into the sump until filled to the designated max fill line. If sand is blown onto rocks or corals use a turkey baster to squirt it to the bottom of the aquarium.

Step 9: Clean or Change Filter Media

Clean all mechanical filter media, including pads, filter socks and cartridges often, and replace them as needed. To clean mechanical media, rinse it under running water until the water running through it is clear (some pads can be squeezed or wrung out.)

If using filter socks, keep extra ones on hand to replace dirty ones. To clean filter socks put them in a washing machine by themselves. Add a quarter cup (less if using a high efficiency washer) of bleach (no additives) to your detergent compartment. Do not use detergent! Once the washing cycle is complete, run the socks through a second rinse cycle with no bleach, just water. Remove socks and let them air dry.

TIP: The more often you clean or replace filter media, the better the water quality of the aquarium. A dirty mechanical filter will eventually lead to increased nitrates as bacteria begin to grow in the media to process the excess waste. It is important to clean and/or replace the physical filter media often.

Replace carbon each month. While it may last longer than a month, it may not, and its life depends on how heavily a reef is stocked. There are many different types of resins that are also helpful in a reef aquarium; if you use any of these, change them according to manufacturer's recommendations.

Step 10: Harvest Algae

When using a refugium to help absorb excess nutrients, harvest part of the macro algae whenever it becomes dense. Trim, thin and remove some macro algae when the compartment is full. If you like, you can change a small amount of water in the refugium to remove detritus from the top of the substrate only. Removing excess algae creates room for more nutrient needing algae to grow and remove excess nutrients from your reef.

CAUTION: Never disturb the sand bed in a refugium. Because there is little or no oxygen in the sand bed, it is a great place for hydrogen sulfide to hide. Disturbing this bed will release this harmful chemical into your aquarium, potentially killing your livestock!

Also the side of the refugium may get covered in micro algae or coralline algae and need to be scraped. The scraping of coralline algae is to view inside the filter therefore all sides do not have to be scraped.

Step 11: Cleaning the Protein Skimmer and Other Equipment

Dump and clean any skimmate (waste) collected in the protein skimmer cup. This waste is usually extremely foul smelling. Clean the collection cup and throat with a bottlebrush. Protein skimmers should be completely taken apart and cleaned every four to six months. For protein skimmers with venturi, clean the venturi regularly to keep salt from building up and reducing airflow.

If using a UV sterilizer, check to be certain the bulb is burning. UV bulbs should be replaced according to the manufacturer suggestions, usually every six to twelve months.

Power heads can be quickly taken apart and cleaned with a small brush every one to three months.

Step 12: Clean the Exterior Glass

Clean outside glass of the aquarium with plain water or an aquarium glass cleaner and a soft rag or paper towel.

Step 13: Clean Inside and Outside the Stand

Wipe down inside and outside of the cabinet or stand. Salt creep buildup can be wiped off with a damp towel or can be vacuumed with a shop vac. **Excess salt creep around hoses and PVC parts may indicate a fitting that needs attention.**

Step 14: Keep a Log or Diary

Keeping a diary or a log is useful for keeping track of water changes. The more consistent you are with water changes, the better the water quality will be for your fish. Filling out a log regularly and recording water tests can also ensure water parameters stay at acceptable levels.

Tracking sheets are handy to keep water changes on track

Livestock Log - This sheet tracks your livestock purchases. When you shop for new fish, corals or invertebrates, take this log with you to ensure your new animal will be compatible with the ones you already have. You can track costs, but the greatest advantage to tracking is so that you can take pride in keeping your fish, corals and invertebrates healthy for years and knowing their ages.

DOWNLOAD YOUR FREE BONUSES: Livestock, Water Testing and Medication Tracking Sheets at http://9nl.be/FreeReefBonuses

Step 15: Clean Light Bulbs and Fixtures

When light bulbs are exposed to saltwater, salt will accumulate on them, cutting down their efficiency. To clean metal halide bulbs and fluorescent and power compact lamps turn them off and unplug them. Let them cool down. It is best to remove the bulbs from their fixture. You can mix freshwater with a small amount of vinegar or rubbing alcohol. Using a soft damp cloth, gently clean bulbs with the mixture and wiping the salt off the bulbs (metal halide manufactures recommend not to touch the bulbs with your hands.) Dry the bulbs and return them to their fixture. If the salt does not come off or is caked on, consider replacing the bulb. If you choose to clean the bulbs while they remain in the fixture above the aquarium, make sure large chunks of salt do not fall onto sea anemones or live corals. Also, if you have a glass or plastic shield protecting the bulbs, keeping it clean will allow a brighter aquarium. Use the same mixture as mentioned above to clean its shield. A razor blade may be necessary to scrape buildup off glass.

Now it is YOUR turn!

Armed with the information you have learned in this guide, you now have a firm foundation and understanding of how to assemble, stock, and care for your own reef aquarium.

You are about to start an amazing adventure by creating your own underwater masterpiece.

Find other books and products by Laurren Schmoyer at http://Aquatic Experts.com.

CLAIM YOUR FREE GIFTS: Thank you for purchasing this saltwater guide. To download your Special FREE Bonuses including useful tracking forms for Livestock, Water Testing and Medication as well as Tips And Solutions For New Reef Hobbyists go to http://9nl.be/FreeReefBonuses

Recommended Reading

Borneman, Eric H., **Aquarium Corals: Selection, Husbandry and Natural History**. Neptune City, NJ: T.F.H. Publications, Edition, 2009. Print.

Calfo, Anthony, **Book of Coral Propagation**. Monroeville, PA: Reading Trees Publication, Second Edition, 2007. Print.

More books by the Author on Amazon

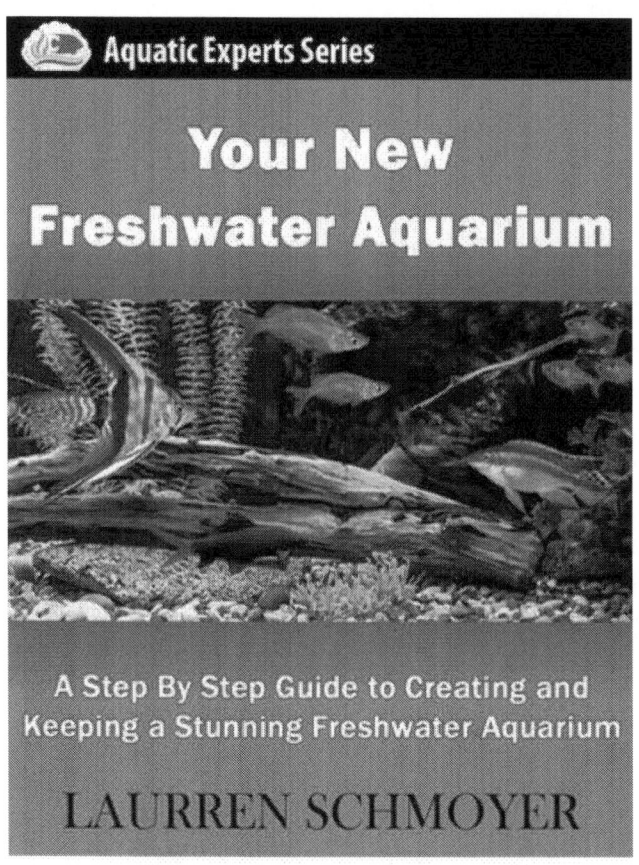

Aquatic Experts Series

Your New Freshwater Aquarium

A Step By Step Guide to Creating and Keeping a Stunning Freshwater Aquarium

LAURREN SCHMOYER

Buy from amazon.com

Have you ever dreamed of owning a beautiful, crystal clear freshwater aquarium filled with schools of lively, graceful fish, with gentle bubbles flowing peacefully behind them? How about enjoying it all with very little care?

You can use Laurren's foolproof, straightforward, easy-to-understand blueprint for setting up, keeping and maintaining your own beautiful aquarium. It is called *Your New Freshwater Aquarium:*

A Step by Step Guide to Creating and Keeping a Stunning Freshwater Aquarium and It ensures a perfect environment to keep your fish healthy and thriving.

In this guide you will learn about the equipment necessary to setup your aquarium; it also includes professional advice on the three types of filtration you must have for your aquarium to thrive. This guide will help take the guess-work out of stocking your new aquarium with examples of fully-stocked aquariums containing hardy, compatible colorful fish for various size aquariums. The guide explains how many fish to add when you first set up your aquarium, when to add more and even what fish can make up a well-stocked aquarium.

You will learn the most efficient way to care for and maintain your aquarium. These are exact techniques and instructions that my professional service technicians use. There are more - tons more -of expert tips throughout the guide.

If you want to create your own beautiful relaxing aquarium stocked with schools of colorful fish and a gentle stream of air bubbles, then you need to order your own copy of *Your New Freshwater Aquarium: A Step by Step Guide to Creating and Keeping a Stunning Freshwater Aquarium* right now!

This saltwater guide is for keeping a larger variety of fish without corals.

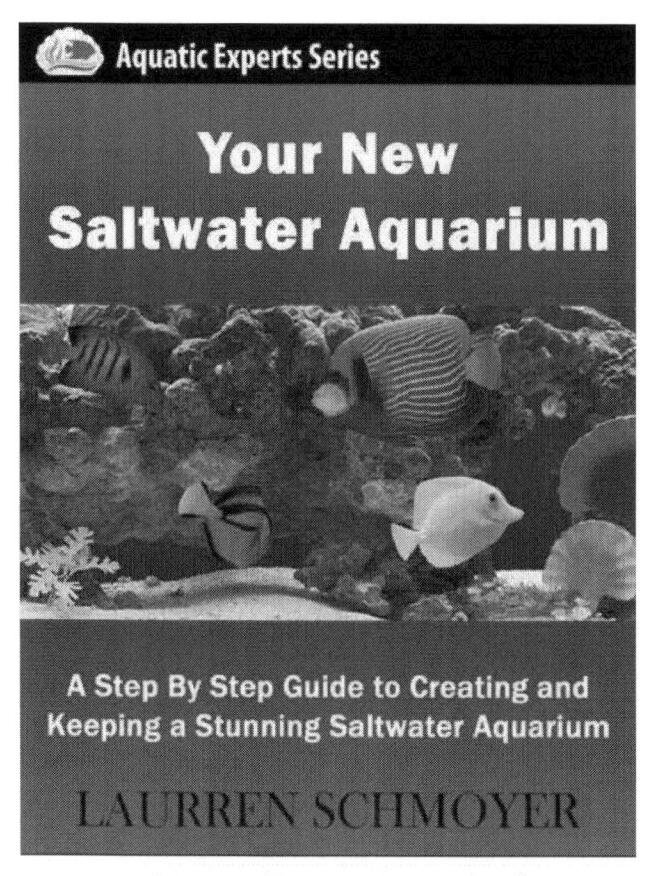

Aquatic Experts Series
Your New Saltwater Aquarium
A Step By Step Guide to Creating and Keeping a Stunning Saltwater Aquarium
LAURREN SCHMOYER

[Buy from amazon.com]

Do You Want A Beautiful Saltwater Filled With Healthy Colorful Exotic Fish?

Keeping bright, colorful, exotic saltwater fish healthy and thriving for years in a saltwater aquarium is the norm for the pros.

Now YOU have the chance to learn how the experts create stunning saltwater aquariums filled with beautiful fish.

Expert Teacher

After over 28 years of working with saltwater aquariums, Laurren Schmoyer has penned his vast experience into a proven system for creating and maintaining amazing underwater paradises. This system guides you through each step, breaking down technical concepts into easy-to-understand language. It is packed with pictures to guide you through each step.

Two Popular Methods

You will find two different approaches to setting up your aquarium. The current trend in saltwater fishkeeping is to set up new saltwater aquariums using live rock, also called FOWLR (Fish-Only-with-Live-Rock). Previously, the traditional method was to decorate with dead corals and/or synthetic decorations. Both practices have their advantages and this guide takes you through a step-by-step process to assembling the saltwater aquarium of your dreams - whichever method you decide.

The Secret to Stacking Live Rock

You will learn the art to stacking live rock so that it creates underwater scenes which mimic ocean reefs. This book teaches you how the pros choose pieces of live rock and how to place and anchor these pieces. You will be able to replicate reef walls with large and small caverns through which fish can swim. You will discover secret techniques of this highly sought-after art.

Now You Too Can Be Confident

Laurren's guide will help you choose a proper filtration system and all the necessary equipment. Learn how to select hardy fish, groups of fish and invertebrates that are compatible with each other, the ins and outs of a quarantine aquarium, and even the safest way to introduce fish into your aquarium. When you have completed these sections, you will feel confident to know which fish will thrive together.

Get Expert Results

You will discover what really keeps these magnificent creatures alive and content for years as well as expert techniques to feeding and caring for your aquarium. This guide removes guesswork; allowing you to have the same amazing results as the pros.

Tips and Techniques to a Thriving Aquarium

This guide will help you build a strong foundation of saltwater knowledge, ensuring a fun and fulfilling fish keeping future. All it takes is the right equipment and expert advice to be able to select healthy fish and keep them thriving in an aquarium.

If you are serious about wanting to create your own stunning underwater paradise, you need to order a copy of "Your New Saltwater Aquarium: A Step By Step Guide To Creating and Keeping A Stunning Saltwater Aquarium" today.

Appendix

How to Cure Rock Taken From the Ocean

Live rock is used to create reef-like structures in both saltwater fish and reef aquariums. Since the rock is collected directly from oceans around the world it is inhabited with algae, animals, plants, bacteria and more. When it is shipped, some of the animal and plant life on the rock are damaged. These rocks must be cured or cleaned before they are safe to put with fish and invertebrates.

The rock arrives in a Styrofoam box and is usually wrapped in wet newspaper to keep it moist. Prepare a bucket of premixed saltwater to a specific gravity between 1.020 and 1.024.

1. Remove the rock from the box carefully. If you wish, wear rubber gloves. Look for any bristleworms that may be hanging partially out of the rock. These worms can sting or bite so use tweezers to remove them.

2. Dip the rock into the bucket of premixed dechlorinated salt water to remove any loose debris. Look for any white, slimy areas or decaying areas. Any decay should be removed with a brush. If you choose to do so, you may remove the algae and plant growth.

3. The rock can be placed into your aquarium or into a holding container while the rock cycles. If you choose to place it in an aquarium no animals may be added until the levels of ammonia and nitrite have dropped back to zero. This can take from 3 to 6 weeks.

4. When placing live rock in an aquarium try to keep as much of the rock off the bottom of the aquarium as possible to ensure good water circulation around the rock. As you build rock walls and cliffs you want as little contact between each piece of rock as possible. This again allows for good circulation and will create great hiding places for the fish.

5. Use powerheads, water pumps and the return pump outlets to direct water flow throughout the rock structure.

6. Make sure your protein skimmer is running properly. It should produce a thick, dark-colored waste in the collection cup. Activated

filter carbon may be used to remove organic waste and the smell. Set the heater between 76° and 78°.

7. The levels of nutrients in the water will begin to rise very rapidly. Keep the aquarium light off. If you keep a light on the aquarium it will grow a lot of unwanted algae.

8. Water changes should be done regularly. While removing the water use a piece of flexible tubing and siphon the white spots or any other dying debris off your rocks when they appear. Also siphon the bottom of the aquarium or container removing any debris. Change at least 50%, up to 100% of the water each time you do a water change. The more often the water changes are done, the lower the waste levels will be and the more plants and animals will survive.

9. When the levels of ammonia and nitrite read zero on your test kit the rock is cycled. Now you can gradually increase the amount of light each day, as well as the amount of time it stays on.

If you have not done a water change recently do one before adding fish, corals or invertebrates.

It takes patience to cure live rock. When the cycle completes, your aquarium will come to life as you begin adding colorful, playful, eye-catching fish, corals and invertebrates!

Glossary

Algae - plant-like organisms that conduct photosynthesis like larger plants, but lack stems, roots and leaves.

Ammonia - (NH_3) - Toxin formed when fish waste and organic matter decompose. Consumed by Nitrosomonas bacteria.

Aragonite - Is found in nature and makes a perfect substrate for saltwater aquariums. As the pH of an aquarium drops below 8.2, aragonite dissolves releasing calcium, trace elements and carbonate. Carbonate is a buffer that keeps your pH up.

Bacteria Starter - Products that contain live cultures of beneficial bacteria used to shorten the Cycle period.

Berlin Filter - an external tank housing the mechanical filtration of a drilled aquarium. Berlin filters often also contain protein skimmers and heaters.

De-chlorinator - Product that removes chlorine from water. Some de-chlorinators also remove ammonia and chloramines.

Filtration - Methods of cleaning/purifying aquarium water. Three major types:
- Mechanical: Physical trapping of suspended particles, accomplished by filter pads or foam.
- Chemical: Trapping of dissolved matter, accomplished with carbon and filter media.
- Biological: Breakdown of harmful compounds, accomplished by beneficial bacteria.

Gravel Vacuum - Siphon tube and hose, used to plunge into gravel to remove detritus.

Heater - Heating element housed in glass or shatter-resistant composite tube. Place the heater near the filter intake to distribute heat evenly.

Hydrometer - An instrument used to measure specific gravity.

Marine snow - Is suspended drifting organic material made up of dead, decaying animals and plants in addition to fecal matter and inorganic dust. At times it can be seen falling from upper waters to the deep ocean floor.

Nitrate (NO_3^-) - End product of Nitrogen Cycle, and least harmful nitrogen compound. Used by plants as fertilizer.

Nitrite (NO_2^-) - Toxin formed from breakdown of ammonia. Consumed by Nitrospira bacteria.

Nitrogen Cycle - Natural process occurring in all living bodies of water - it is the breakdown of organic matter and waste products into ammonia, then nitrite, then nitrate.

Nitrosomonas - Beneficial bacteria that consume toxic ammonia.

Nitrospira - Beneficial bacteria that consumes toxic nitrite.

PAR Meter - A PAR (Photo-synthetically Active Radiation) meter measures the light in a reef to ensure the proper wavelengths for corals at particular depths in the aquarium. Once we know the PAR value, we have a better idea of what types of corals to select as well as general placement in a reef aquarium.

pH - Measure of how acidic or basic a solution is on a scale from 0-14. Numbers below seven indicate acid, seven is neutral, and numbers above seven indicate base.

Sessile Invertebrates - Invertebrates which attach or anchor themselves in one place. Good examples are barnacles, corals and sponges.

Specific Gravity - The ratio of the mass of a solid or liquid to the mass of an equal volume of distilled water at 4°C (39°F). In a saltwater aquarium we measure specific gravity with a hydrometer and change it by adding either salt or water to get a reading of 1.020 to 1.025. This reading will change with temperature variations.

Stalk - Is an elongated, cylindrical part of a coral which supports the coral polyp.

Sump - a holding tank that goes below an aquarium. It can be made of plastic, glass or acrylic. Water is routed from an aquarium down to fill the sump. Then a pump is placed in the sump to pump the water back to the aquarium. The sump holds equipment such as protein skimmer, heaters, etc.

Wet/Dry Filter - an external tank housing the mechanical and biological filtration of a drilled aquarium. Wet/dry filters often also contain protein skimmers and heaters.

More About the Author

Laurren Schmoyer at age 13 got his first job at a pet store. His love for animals prompted his study in Biology at University of North Carolina at Greensboro. After graduating from college, he searched for a career he could enjoy. Keeping fish aquariums both as a hobby and a job seemed like the ideal solution; Laurren opened an aquarium service company and began servicing aquariums in the Greensboro area. Immediately his phone started ringing with simple fish-keeping questions. Laurren felt the area needed a knowledgeable aquarium store. Armed with ambition, no money and a baby on the way he decided to create one. In a family-owned space, the tiny fish store materialized.

Since these meager beginnings, Aquamain's Fish World grew into one of the largest aquarium stores on the east coast. Laurren grew his small retail aquarium store of 1,500 square feet into a 10,000 square foot superstore. After 25 years, Laurren left Aquamain's Fish World, taking with him the aquarium service clients and opened a new aquarium service company to pursue a different adventure. He has spent many years teaching and training his customers in the experts' way to keep fish, plants, invertebrates and corals healthy and thriving for years. His desire and passion is to share his knowledge so that anyone can be a successful hobbyist. He now spends his time writing books, pet magazine articles and continues to create informative videos and other educational products. His products can be found at http://AquaticExperts.com.

Printed in Great Britain
by Amazon.co.uk, Ltd.,
Marston Gate.